# Health Preserver

# Health Preserver
## Defining the Versatility of Vitamin E

# by Wilfrid E. Shute, M.D.

featuring special chapters by Dr. Shute's daughters,
Karen Shute Berry and Barbara Shute Carnahan

Rodale Press, Emmaus, PA

**Library of Congress Cataloging in Publication Data**

Shute, Wilfrid E      1907-
   Health preserver.
   Includes index.
   1.   Vitamin E.   2. Health.   I.   Berry, Karen Shute, joint author.   II.   Carnahan, Barbara Shute, joint author.   III.   Title.   [DNLM:   1.   Vitamin E—Therapeutic use—Popular works.   QU179 S56h]
   RM666.T65S5125      615'.328      77-14086
   ISBN  0-87857-189-2

Printed in the United States of America on recycled paper.

      6   8   10   9   7   5      hardcover

DEPOSIT TICKET

NINA RATTRAY
1318 KOSTLAND AVENUE
BROOKLYN, NY 11236

DATE _____ 19___

This deposit is accepted subject to verification and to our rules and regulations

| | CASH | DOLLARS | CENTS |
|---|---|---|---|
| C | | | |
| H | | | |
| E | | | |
| C | | | |
| K | | | |
| S | | | |
| | | | |
| LIST CHECKS SINGLY | | | |
| TOTAL | | 83 | |

TOTAL ITEMS

0000682 LAST INT PD 9.9
005 09MAY83

***200.00

***2402.43 BAL
****200.00 CDP

# Contents

# Introduction

This new book on the therapeutic uses of vitamin E came about as a way to celebrate vitamin E's amazing versatility. For many pathological conditions in humans, vitamin E is an essential part of successful treatment, and, for some ailments, it is the only effective therapy known. The list of uses grows as more and more physicians discover that, in the proper dose range, vitamin E is indeed a potent weapon in both the prevention and the treatment of various ills that beset their patients.

Vitamin E is acknowledged as absolutely essential for the life of every cell in the body, and it is generally agreed among physiologists that an adequate concentration of this substance must be present for the normal function of each cell. So I am not out to reestablish its standing as a vitamin. In this book I am concerned only with the therapeutic actions of vitamin E when it is used at many times the minimum daily requirement set by the government authorities.

The tocopherols are the active elements in vitamin E and alpha tocopherol is by far the most active of these. For all practical purposes, alpha tocopherol is responsible for the therapeutic action attributed to vitamin E. Therefore, alpha tocopherol and vitamin E are used interchangeably in this book.

I am also pleased to include the chapters by my daughters, Barbara and Karen. In their respective professions as speech therapist and nurse they have found effective ways to use vitamin E in treating problems that appeared hopeless to other professionals. Perhaps their experiences will prompt others to discover new facets of this remarkable healing agent.

# Answering Some Basic Questions About Vitamin E

*We have come to expect a great deal from vitamin E, and we are rarely disappointed when we try it in treating all manner of ailments. This very success has led to confusion and skepticism on the part of the lay public and the medical profession. How, they ask, can the same substance be useful against heart disease, diabetes, and skin problems? In short, it sounds too good to be true!*

*The secret of vitamin E's remarkable powers lies in the fact that it is a basic element in the body's make-up. When it is lacking, fundamental bodily functions are adversely affected. Supplementary vitamin E merely provides the body with what it needs to run properly, protect itself from disease, or heal itself if injury or disease should strike. This section will explain, in detail, what I mean.*

1

## Why Vitamin E Is Able to Do So Much for You

To understand why vitamin E is effective in treating so many physical ailments in man, it is necessary to realize how many functions it has in the body. Its influence becomes clear when we see that sufficient vitamin E is essential to the most basic body systems, and when it is missing they are certain to break down. Increase vitamin E intake, and the process is sure to be reversed.

Obviously, blood must always remain fluid in the heart and blood vessels, down to the smallest capillary. A normal concentration of vitamin E in the bloodstream works to prevent clotting there. Conversely, with cuts and bruises and serious injury, blood must clot outside the blood vessels and in the ends of severed vessels. Vitamin E does not interfere with this development, for it is not a "blood thinner" and never causes excessive hemorrhage. As the chief antithrombin (anticlotting agent), its major function is to keep the blood from clotting *inside* the blood vessels.

The other main action of vitamin E is reducing the oxygen requirement of the body's tissues. Cells function properly only when the blood supply to them is within a certain normal range, and when it delivers all the essential vitamins, amino acids, trace minerals, *and oxygen* to them in necessary amounts. (Of course, the blood's ability to remove the cells' waste products is also vital.)

Whenever a cell is completely deprived of oxygen, it dies. If its oxygen supply falls below a critical level, but not so low that the cell can no longer survive, the cell will begin to act abnormally. With enough vitamin E, the cell may regain its normal function because that vitamin decreases the need for oxygen in the cell.

With certain types of damage to a cell, nature overdoes its response to the injury. The local blood supply is increased; the capillaries dilate and allow some of the blood's elements to leak out into the tissues. This is usually a very valuable reaction—for example, as a means of combating infections. However, in some situations this increased capillary permeability is harmful. In effect, it floods the tissues with fluid and slows down the passage of oxygen across the cell membranes, and this may actually prevent the cells from resisting the damaging agent.

Vitamin E restores normal capillary permeability in such cases. The fluids return to the vessels, oxygen in adequate quantities returns to the cells, and the body is equipped to repel the damaging agent. This explains the rapid resolution of such threats as acute rheumatic fever and nephritis when vitamin E therapy is instituted in the very early stages of these two diseases.

Most extensive burns, as well as wounds in which large areas of skin are lost, are routinely grafted as soon as possible. This is a long and always painful process because of two characteristics of scar tissue: contraction and tenderness. In the healing process scar tissue contracts, leading to deformity and to some interference with the normal range of movement, particularly when the area involves underarms, groin, elbows, knees, or the skin of the neck. Also, scar tissue is tender and often painful to the touch. It sometimes forms excessively, becoming heaped up, red, and itchy.

When vitamin E is used, any scars which do appear contract very little or not at all, and are not tender. Vitamin E prevents scar tissue from heaping up, or if that has already occurred, vitamin E will take away the redness and the itchiness. Often vitamin E diminishes old, unsightly scars.

Vitamin E has a bacteriostatic (bacteria-limiting) action which is most useful in treating large burns and other large denuded areas, recent or chronic. For example, it allows the old, infected bases of chronic varicose ulcers to throw off the gross infection and, along with its oxygen-conservation abilities, vitamin E promotes the formation of healthy granulation tissue over which skin can grow and spread. Such healthy granulation tissue can sustain the life and growth of the skin cells falling on it from the surrounding intact skin surfaces. Many such ulcers heal by this type of self-grafting.

Vitamin E dilates small capillaries, speeding up their extension into granulation tissue, and into the edges of chronic ulcers. It also accelerates the opening up of collateral vessels around areas of major vessels, whether arteries or veins, that have become narrowed.

# How to Use Vitamin E Intelligently

Like every other successful agent, vitamin E has its own peculiarities, its own drawbacks, and its own range of usefulness. Timetables for expected results vary considerably; so do optimum dosages. Much depends on the situation.

For example, the successful treatment with vitamin E of edema and hemolytic anemia in premature infants depends upon the use of a standardized potent product in the 75- to 100-IU range. The response follows a recognizable time schedule which is about the same as that in the treatment of the average heart case with appropriate dosage. Usually, the first indication of response in a heart case is seen in seven to ten days, but it may not be really well developed for four to six weeks. The edema and all associated symptoms in the infants respond completely in a month to six weeks.

By contrast, the response to vitamin E of the patient suffering from acute thrombophlebitis, acute nephritis, or an acute rheumatic fever may be obvious in two to four days. The maximum vitamin dosage used may be as much as 4,800 IU a day, though 800 to 1,600 IU a day will usually give a full response.

Then, there are certain definite precautions that must be observed in vitamin E therapy. It is of great importance and very successful in the treatment of chronic rheumatic heart disease, and also in the treatment of hypertensive heart disease when used correctly. However, improperly used, vitamin E can be ineffectual as a treatment for these ailments, and very dangerous. Anyone using vitamin E therapy must understand this, and carefully follow a specific mode of treatment.

The patient with an elevated blood pressure and with heart involvement can nearly always be treated satisfactorily with vitamin E, *provided* his blood pressure is being treated and is under control. It is generally wisest to begin such patients on a small quantity of vitamin E until its effect on the blood pressure and on the therapeutic blood pressure control can be evaluated.

Vitamin E usually enhances the effect of the agents used to reduce pressure. The same is true when using digitalis. It is especially important to be aware of this when using digitalis in treating heart patients, since vitamin E potentiates the action of this very useful, but hazardous drug.

When iron in medicine form comes into contact with vitamin E it neutralizes the vitamin, a fact known almost since the vitamin was first recognized and used experimentally. Infants being fed with prediluted commercial formulas are prime candidates for vitamin E shortages, since these products often have iron added by the manufacturer. The added iron steals a share of the babies' original supply of vitamin E. Infants on breast milk generally maintain normal serum tocopherol (vitamin E) levels; those on artificial formula tend to have low levels.

Mineral oil dissolves vitamin E and does not readily release it to the body.

Estrogen (the female hormone) and vitamin E are antagonists, and a review of the uses of estrogen is long overdue. Estrogen can be dangerous and, in the field of heart problems, is very seldom indicated.

Very rarely, a patient is allergic to one or the other of the three forms of vitamin E on the market. The difficulty here is that often this is not evident until after prolonged use, or when a patient who has been taking E for months takes an increased dose. Fortunately, changing the type of vitamin E solves the problem nearly every time.

There are several substances which are not only compatible with vitamin E, but which act to increase the value of it. Notable among them are megadoses of vitamin C and appropriate amounts of the B complex. Thyroid extract is also in this category, when used in suitable situations.

The combination of vitamin E and the trace element selenium has long been used to advantage in the treatment of white muscle disease in animals, especially the lamb and the calf. Vitamin E by itself will effect a cure if used soon enough in many cases. Selenium is even more effective in that it rescues a slightly larger percentage of the young animals. However, selenium is toxic and vitamin E is not. If the two are combined they reinforce each other and much smaller quantities of each can be used with no toxic effects. The combination is much more effective than either alone—about 97 percent of the affected young animals are cured.

H. E. Burns, D.V.M., has manufactured this combination product for years, in a capsule named Seletoc®, containing sodium selenite (equivalent to one mg. of selenium), 2.19 mg. and vitamin E (as d-alpha tocopherol acid succinate), 68 IU, an injectible form of the same strength.

Several million doses of Seletoc® have been given to animals. In addition to white muscle disease in sheep and cattle, it has been used for symptomatic relief of clinical signs associated with lameness in dogs. E. W. Kienholz now reports in *Lancet* (531, 1975) that Seletoc® has been successfully used in the treatment of certain knee problems, chondromalacia patillae, and other types of ligament irritation in the human.

Human milk contains six times as much alpha tocopherol and twice as much selenium as cow's milk.

If indeed selenium proves an important therapeutic and prophylactic agent in human medicine, its success will probably depend upon a product combining it with vitamin E. Both together are apparently more effective than either one alone. The vitamin E makes it possible to use an adequate quantity of selenium without the dangers of toxicity.

When steroids must be used as a treatment, their effective dosage can be reduced by as much as two-thirds, if the patient is taking vitamin E. The vitamin limits the side effects of the steroids, increases their effectiveness, and permits the eventual reduction, or even cessation, of maintenance doses.

One must remember to *tailor the dose* to the circumstance. Anything useful can be dangerous under specific conditions. Insulin has prolonged many lives, but has killed a lot of patients when incorrectly used. The antibiotics have been effective agents, but have caused many serious reactions, some worse than the disease. Digitalis, for many years the only useful heart drug, is risky and frequently misused; it can and does kill.

Vitamin E is much safer than any of these, yet it, too, must be used wisely.

# How Vitamin E Has Proven Itself Through Its Effect on Animals

Scientists traditionally use animals for their initial experiments in testing new drugs or new forms of treatment. The animals' responses may well be reproducible in humans, with appropriate adjustment of the dosage. One advantage in using animals for testing is their relative immunity to the powers of suggestion. This adds to the validity of positive results achieved in using vitamin E to treat diseases, proving it is not a case of mind over matter, as was suggested concerning the following experience.

My brother and I were called before the Ontario College of Physicians and Surgeons to explain our "use of vitamin E in *curing* heart disease." We replied that we would be happy to appear before this governing body to explain our "use of vitamin E in the *treatment* of heart disease."

At the meeting of the Ontario College, Dr. Edward Bartram, then Chief of Cardiology at the University of Western Ontario (London), told them that he had not seen a patient of ours whose improvement could not be explained by the forceful personalities of the Shutes attending them. This was a curious statement, as I promptly pointed out to the assembly, since our second patient was *in extremis,* with a maximum degree of edema and heart failure, and of all things, was one of Dr. Bartram's patients. Moreover, the doctor had seen this man on the day he was first given vitamin E and Dr. Bartram had said there was nothing more that he could do, and that it was too bad the patient was so clear, mentally, because he would die. The man eventually returned to work and to playing in London's Little Theatre Orchestra. This on vitamin E—plus my brother's "forceful personality!"

When dealing with animals, such questions of suggestion don't arise. Dr. R. H. Lambert, at the time president of the Irish Veterinary Association and often published in the veterinary journals in England and the United States, picked up Evan's initial reports and began to try vitamin E in his practice, particularly on dogs and cats. His results deserve consideration, for he showed that dogs in deep congestive heart failure could be returned to the hunting field to do a full day's work, that old and failing dogs and cats could be restored to relatively youthful activities, and that racing greyhounds could be greatly improved in performance.

Dr. Lambert continued to use vitamin E in his small-animal practice and reported on continuing successes at the Third International Congress on Vitamin E, held in Venice, Italy, in 1955. (See *Proceedings of the Congress,* p.610.) In *World Medicine* (July 14, 1971) there is a report of an interview with Dr. Lambert in which he said, "I have written several papers on the subject (the use of vitamin E in animals). Since writing these papers I have verified my findings in each case many hundreds of times. I am convinced that natural vitamin E is the most valuable drug on the market. It is rightly called the 'versatile vitamin'."

In Canada, the leading breeder of race horses has been using vitamin E under rigid scientific control and supervision by his veterinarian, and his results show in the improvement of his horses' records in the breeding stables, in both stallions and mares.

As a successful breeder and exhibitor and as a long-time licensed judge of dog shows in Canada and the United States, also Bermuda and Venezuela, I have had rather unusual opportunities in the realm of vitamin E in show dogs. I have seen the results in many dogs owned by others as well as those I have bred or owned. I, too, have seen old, senile dogs regain their youth through vitamin E, have healed intractable sores and ulcers in show dogs with it; have helped cure, and I mean cure, the unduly common rear-end paralysis of over fifty dachshunds. And I have read in the official magazine of the American Kennel Club the results of vitamin E in making a thin, nervous Old English sheep dog into a champion, shown in good show condition.

A particularly interesting experience occurred some years ago after I had judged at a show in Ontario and had given an award to a particularly fine young collie. The owner came up to remind me that she had consulted me some three years before about their old champion who had become so rheumatic that he could hardly get to his feet and occasionally had to be helped up. Using vitamin E on him at my suggestion, the old dog not only became free of pain and disability, but he was the sire of the collie I had chosen that day!

"Tying up" in horses is analogous to intermittent claudication in humans, and it responds to vitamin E. So does Scottie cramp, a condition in Scottish terriers in which they develop a cramp in one or both hind legs after running a little way. In 1955, I solved the problem with vitamin E in a little Scottie bitch of top show quality, bred and owned by one of the largest Scottie kennels in the mid-west. A similar case was reported in the *Veterinary Record* (68: 411, 1956) by a veterinarian, J. O. Joshua in England: ". . . A two-year-old Scottish terrier bitch had Scottie cramp. On 100 IU (of vitamin E) a day she gradually improved. Before treatment, cramp developed after 200 yards exercise, after treatment she could run a mile and a half."

Many of this country's top kennels use vitamin E routinely, and two owners have told me they couldn't run their kennels successfully without it. Many began to use vitamin E as a result of the following report published in *Dog World* (April, 1967), a popular magazine devoted to dogs:

### Lack of Vitamin E Leads to Widest Variety of Disorders

Perhaps the largest variety of body disorders associated with nutritional deficiency of any single vitamin results from a shortage of vitamin E, states David C. Herting, Ph.D., in the *Journal of Clinical Nutrition*. Vitamin E deficiency affects the reproductive system (testicular degeneration, defective development of the embryo); the muscular system (skeletal muscular dystrophy, cardiac necrosis and fibrosis, etc.); the circulatory system (anemias); the skeletal system (incisor depigmentation); and the nervous system. In addition, vitamin E deficiency may be manifested by a number of other conditions such as dissolved fatty tissue, lung hemorrhage, etc. It is also pertinent to note, states the good doctor, that vitamin E has been found to ameliorate the adverse effects of various toxic agents and a number of suboptimal dietary and environmental conditions.

**Fertility and Pregnancy**   Vitamin E has long been considered necessary in animal husbandry and in fur farming. Mink breeders, for example, know that adding vitamin E to the ration produces an average of one and a half kits more per litter over mink not supplemented.

When my father and older brother Evan first used vitamin E in treating human obstetrical and gynecological problems, the results obtained were very uneven, ranging from very good to fair to zero. Their work was not taken seriously by the profession because attempts to reproduce promising results were seldom successful. Eventually they discovered that the products others used in testing—wheat germ oil capsules stored on drugstore shelves and used in minuscule quantities—were virtually inert.

After much investigation they discovered that to achieve relatively consistent results the wheat germ oil had to be made from a specific type of wheat germ by the cold-pressed process, then kept cold and used fresh in large doses. With this product, the results showing vitamin E as a useful factor in treating obstetrical and gynecological problems warranted reporting in medical journals.

When a synthetic vitamin E became available in 1941 it was possible, for the first time, to prescribe an exact amount of alpha tocopherol, the most potent part of vitamin E. Results became more dependable and predictable. The percentage of cases of *abruptio placentae* (premature detachment of the placenta from the wall of the uterus) successfully carried to term, increased. Also, many women previously considered sterile, produced babies, much to their delight and that of their husbands. The vitamin E treatment was gratifyingly effective against such menopausal symptoms as vaginitis and vulvitis.

The success of Evan and my other obstetrician-gynecologist brother, Wallace, in these areas, brought them not only local but international fame and honors.

I have used vitamin E successfully in returning a valuable old, sterile male Doberman pinscher to full potency. He sired litters of four, eight, and twelve in his next three matings.

In another case, one of the top champion-producing sires of all times had been sterile for some time before I chanced to visit his owner. On vitamin E he was returned to normal fertility and sired several champions during his final years.

I have twice been consulted about male dogs who ignored a female in full season. Each would take a sniff and then go away and lie down. On vitamin E, both dogs showed normal interest, took full advantage of their next opportunity, and both became potent champion-producing sires.

I have corresponded with two people whose old favorite dogs, one a Great Dane, the other a terrier, developed serious kidney diseases. Both responded to vitamin E therapy.

Our own two house dogs—an eleven-year-old miniature poodle, male, and a six-year-old champion female Doberman pinscher—were started on 200 IU of vitamin E a day, at my wife's suggestion. The poodle was her dog and failing badly. Indeed, we had him at our summer cottage and expected we would have to bury him there. When we did get him home to the city he was literally almost dead. On vitamin E he was soon well, acting like a six-months-old puppy, and lived six more years to be seventeen years old. The Doberman was started on vitamin E only because she was there, but she, too, regained her youthful bounce and activity and lived a full and extended life.

**The Aging Process**   Body cells are constantly being worn out and replaced. Cells can reproduce outside the body on a culture medium. These tissue cultures constitute a useful way to measure the effect of different substances, directly on cells. However, there is a specific limit to the number of cell multiplications that can be obtained. After a certain number of cell divisions, usually about fifty, the process comes to a dead halt. So far, nothing known will increase the number of such cell divisions except vitamin E. With vitamin E added to the culture, the cells reproduce through the 120th generation. This experiment was reported from the Lawrence Berkeley Laboratory in California. It may explain why white rats getting vitamin E supplementation show a definitely increased life span. It has been suggested that vitamin E can slow down the aging process in humans.

Dr. Linus Pauling has made an interesting point in this regard. He has shown that adequate supplementation of all vitamins—especially several grams a day of vitamin C and about 1,200 IU of vitamin E—and of trace minerals, will not only help to prolong most lives but, of greater importance perhaps, will increase the length of happy, useful, enjoyable, efficient years.

# Modern Living Demands More Vitamin E

*Why do we suddenly need to take supplementary vitamin E, when we got along for thousands of years without taking any extra? It's a reasonable question and it is often asked of me. The answer is equally reasonable, I think. Two things have happened to change the traditional picture: we get less vitamin E than in any age before, and we need more vitamin E than any people ever needed before. The first is due to modern methods of food processing, the second results from the fantastic developments we've seen in industry and transportation. I believe the following pages will convince you that I'm right.*

# Environment

Because of the concentration of industrial plants in our cities, plus ever-increasing numbers of automobiles and planes, our air has a higher-than-ever concentration of noxious chemicals in it, and many of these are irritating to the air passages and lungs. The long-term effects are probably very serious.

Two of the main irritants have been identified as ozone and nitrogen dioxide, both damaging to lung tissue. In animal experiments, vitamin E given in both nutrition doses and therapeutic doses has shown ability to protect the lungs against these agents.

At a Chicago meeting of the Vitamin Information Bureau Seminar in 1975, Dr. Daniel B. Menzel, formerly of the Battelle Institute and now director of pharmacology and of medicine at Duke University in Durham, North Carolina, reported on the value of vitamin E in protecting human lungs against air pollutants. Dr. Menzel applied the knowledge gained in the rat experiments to humans, but he found that it took at least 200 IU of vitamin E a day to reverse the damage to humans' lungs from pollutants.

Dr. James W. Gillett of the Department of Agricultural Chemistry at Oregon State University, reported that pesticides deplete the body's supply of vitamin E. Apparently, the vitamin E is used up in the process of detoxifying the contaminant.

Three years ago, my wife and I had extensive physical examinations in a famous California clinic. Among the tests run was one for heavy metals contamination, including lead. Of the several thousands who had been tested in this clinic, we were the first who showed no contamination whatever. Since no one else who visited that clinic had taken vitamin E in clinical dosages for over thirty years, this raised the question of whether or not our protection was due to vitamin E. We thought of a simple way to check this.

A friend of ours living in the Los Angeles area had had a coronary occlusion twelve years before and had immediately started to take 1,600 IU or more of vitamin E per day. We persuaded him to have all the same tests we had; to our great delight he, too, showed no evidence of heavy metal contamination, although he had lived in the heavily polluted Los Angeles area for many years.

*Medical World News* (June 2, 1974) reported a release from the Department of Agriculture describing an experiment in which rats, given lead in their drinking water and insufficient amounts of vitamin E in their food, developed enlarged spleens, anemia, and more fragile red blood cells than those animals also poisoned by lead, who got enough vitamin E. Dr. Henry Dymsza of the University of Rhode Island reported that there were no adverse effects and even slightly better growth rate in the animals who got up to 1,000 times the "normal" amount of vitamin E.

People living "normal" lives in today's environment are subjected to so many different toxic substances in air and water, and so many chemicals in food—many of which seem to be countered by vitamin E intake—that, in my opinion, virtually everyone needs to take it as a daily supplement and in a fair-sized quantity, 200 to 800 IU as a minimum.

## Polyunsaturated Fats and Heart Protection

I also believe that the harm done by those who advocate increasing the proportion of polyunsaturated fats and restricting animal fats in the diet, is incalculable. Dr. Hans Nieper, winner of the Nobel Prize for his original work on the cobalt treatment for cancer, introduced me to a paper published in the German journal, *Arztliche Praxis* (November, 1971), which showed that while arteriosclerosis of the coronary arteries supplying the heart had remained substantially unchanged during this century, clots in the coronary arteries, the so-called "heart attack" first described in 1912, had increased slowly but steadily until the general acceptance of the polyunsaturated fats idea. At that time it began a precipitous increase which has continued.

The suggestion that these low-cholesterol products contain enough vitamin E to protect the body from the polyunsaturated fat menace is not true. First, the form of the vitamin E occurring naturally in these oils and margarines is not the potent alpha fraction, so it is virtually useless. Second, a large proportion of the oils, if not all, come out of Eastman Kodak Company or General Mills where the vitamin E is taken out of them to be sold separately.

A most unfortunate aspect of this problem is the American Heart Association's activity in pushing the idea of restricting animal fats, along with the addition of polyunsaturates as a protection against arteriosclerosis and heart disease in children, even in the new-born. *Nutrition Today* (January-February, 1975) presents a thorough summary of the question, showing the lack of any definite evidence for this view.

More and more pediatricians are placing babies on formulas high in polyunsaturated fats without supplementing these formulas with additional vitamin E, something which must always be done. Increasing numbers of babies are developing hemolytic anemia and the incidence of sudden crib deaths is also increasing. In my opinion, both are the result of this type of feeding.

This same foolish idea is now affecting most of the population according to a 1971 report made by Dr. Nicholas R. D. Luzio of the Tulane University School of Medicine to the American Chemical Society. He stated that diene fats were detected in the blood plasma of seventy-eight out of eighty-one persons tested. These diene fats, characteristic of polyunsaturated fats, are oxidized in the body to form peroxidized fats unless an antioxidant, such as vitamin E, is present in sufficient amounts to prevent this transformation. The peroxidized lipids formed from the diene fats are toxic to various cells and contribute to certain disease states. Vitamin E significantly lowers the level of dienes in the blood.

The answer is fewer polyunsaturates and more vitamin E intake, certainly much more than the two-to-eight IU a day current in most American diets. Dr. Menzel of Duke University suggests a 200 IU daily supplement of vitamin E for everyone and M. K. Horwitt, Ph.D., professor of biochemistry, St. Louis University, School of Medicine, St. Louis, Missouri, originally responsible for setting the Recommended Daily Amount of five to thirty units a day, now suggests 800 IU a day as a safe supplement.

# How the Astronauts Demonstrated the Need for a Steady Supply of Vitamin E

The astronauts returned surprisingly tired and weakened from the fourteen-day Gemini VII flight of December 4, 1965. The puzzled examining doctors found that the men had lost approximately 25 percent of their red blood cells during the flight. Dr. David Turner suggested that the loss was due to a deficiency of vitamin E in the diet provided for the men. Without sufficient vitamin E the fat portion of the red blood cell membrane quickly lost its protective oxygen, which means the integrity of the membrane was destroyed, and consequently the hemoglobin leaked out.

In a television interview, Dr. Turner stated that he happened to think of vitamin E deficiency as the cause because he had been doing postgraduate work in London, Ontario, at the time two doctors there "achieved a measure of notoriety" for their work on vitamin E as an antioxidant. My wife Dorothy and I happened to tune in on this interview and I was glad to learn that the work of my brother Evan and I was probably responsible for finding the solution to one of the astronauts' problems.

The truly remarkable part of this affair is that the Aerospace Medical Association at a meeting in Miami, Florida on May 13, 1964 had already decided that every astronaut going into outer space should have a diet fortified with vitamin E. Obviously the idea had not yet been implemented. But from then on the men returned to earth with their hemoglobin and red cells intact, with the help of vitamin E. Also they were free of the fatigue suffered by those who had preceded them.

Dr. Turner's observation confirmed a statement I often make: a patient taking therapeutic doses of vitamin E daily cannot afford to stop or he loses virtually all of the vitamin E and all of its protective action in about three days. Clearly, the astronauts were in serious trouble without their vitamin E during that period in space. One-quarter of their red blood cells had been destroyed after just fourteen days.

What are we to think of the statement made ten years later by Dr. A. L. Tappel in *Nutrition Today* (July-August, 1973): "Many months of deprivation (of vitamin E) would have to pass in order to deplete the body stores."?

## Vitamin E's Role in Treating Today's Special Behavioral Problems

As you will see in a later chapter, my daughter Barbara used vitamin E, 800 IU a day, in turning four problem children she treated into relatively normal ones, able to rejoin, keep up with, and compete with children of their own age in a normal school environment. Otherwise their futures were not bright, and each may well have joined the increasing number of school drop-outs, perhaps on their way to becoming juvenile delinquents or even worse.

Similarly, the four-year-old boy my younger daughter, Karen, describes in her chapter was probably headed for a serious emotional problem. The removal of refined sugar and starches was effective in his return to near normal, but he was also given 800 IU of vitamin E a day and I am convinced that it was equally important.

Dr. Ben Feingold of the Kaiser Permanente group in the San Francisco area of California, became interested in the problem of hyperkinesia and learning difficulties in children as an outgrowth of his practice in allergy. A woman he was treating for giant hives responded promptly to a specific diet which eliminated artificial food colors and flavors. However, this patient had also been under psychiatric care for two years, had been hostile and aggressive, unable to get along with her husband, her family, and her coworkers. Her psychiatric symptoms cleared on this diet in less than two weeks.

Dr. Feingold cites a California study showing an increase in hyperkinesia (hyperactivity) and learning difficulties in the last ten years from 2 percent to an average of 20 percent to 25 percent, and in some places 40 percent of the entire school population. These problems occur mostly in boys (another study says in a proportion of nine to one), usually in only one child in a family, and bear no relationship to the child's I.Q. or the socioeconomic status of the family.

Dr. Feingold has successfully treated some of these children with a salicylate-free diet which eliminates 80 percent of the food additives, including the artificial flavors and colors. He reports a 55 percent success.

Most of these cases are related to trouble with carbohydrate metabolism, to the use of refined carbohydrates and starches. Dr. Feingold eliminates the sugars and makes sure that the children's general nutrition is adequate, especially with respect to their vitamins and trace minerals.

So here is a seemingly insurmountable problem, yet one which must somehow be solved. The increase in juvenile delinquency is probably due to the increase in the number of children who cannot learn, no matter how much they try and no matter how much their parents and teachers may want them to. The children cannot continue on to a higher education; they may well be unable to hold a job of any kind, and may even turn to alcohol or drugs.

Several reports show that vitamin E can evoke a positive change in some cases of mental deficiency. One of these unexpectedly resulted while a researcher was studying the effect of vitamin E on a rare skin disease in two brothers, as reported in the *Canadian Medical Association Journal* (June 6, 1964). The doctor noted that the patients' mental attitudes improved along with their skin condition.

Doctors at the Ontario Hospital School, Orillia, Ontario, investigated the influence of vitamin E therapy on three groups of twenty mentally retarded boys, divided by age. In each group half of the subjects were in the moron group and half in the idiot or imbecile group. "As early as two weeks after treatment began, some intellectual and behavioral improvement was noted by the teachers in half of their subjects." The best response was in the ten- to thirteen-year-old group receiving 1,200 IU of vitamin E a day. "The fact that these patients were brighter, more alert, and more cooperative made their care and management easier," said the report in the *American Journal of Mental Deficiency* (69, no. 3, 1961).

We have shown that vitamin E is effective in treating some cases of abnormal mentality. A hypoglycemic diet is also effective in many cases. Removing all artificial colors and flavors from the diet of children improves many cases. A combined treatment using all this knowledge should be most effective and needs intensive attention.

The answer has to come from the "grass roots" level. The mothers of this country must be made aware of the problem and must act. They must change their eating habits, and those of their children. Children, school boards, teachers, and public health officials must become aware of the role of nutrition and must act.

Currently, there is a belated interest in nutrition among doctors. However, you must remember that few doctors have had contact with even the basic elements of adequate nutrition. Until recently, they have had no training in nutrition in medical schools, no course in nutrition. Now, at least in some medical schools, students do get a few hours on the subject.

**Athletic Performance**    If we are to see a change for the better in the behavioral and social attitudes of today's youngsters, their achievements in sports will certainly encourage it. Adequate intake of vitamin E will help them to win. There are numerous examples of its power to improve athletic performance.

"The Chicago Black Hawks Are Hooked on Vitamin E." This was the title of an article in *Hockey Illustrated* (May, 1973). The Detroit Red Wings in their halcyon days also found it useful. The Russians reported a controlled trial of vitamin E supplementation in their cross-country skiers and cyclists, and found that they could estimate quite accurately the optimum amount of the nutrient necessary for various types of athletic activities. Essentially, vitamin E proved more useful for events demanding prolonged athletic exertion than for those of short duration. Since that report appeared, Russian athletes have dominated much of the international sports scene.

Years ago, I supervised the use of vitamin E supplementation in Canada's champion swimming team. During this time the club won many titles and championships. It was easy to measure the improvement that was due to vitamin E, since these athletes were in constant and consistent training. We could even manipulate the times of the top four in any event by the giving or withholding of vitamin E, or varying the dosage level. Other swim clubs have reported the success of megavitamin E in improving athletic performance. My daughter, Karen, a world record holder in age-group swimming, was one of the stars of this club.

Otto and Maria Jelinek, world pairs skating champions, were also under my care. Three weeks before the Olympics at Squaw Valley, they had difficulty completing their five-minute routine in practice sessions at Oakville, Ontario, because of shortness of breath. Figure skating becomes more complicated and difficult every year, and their routine was very vigorous. On 1,600 IU of vitamin E a day they had no difficulty finishing their routine, followed almost immediately by a two-minute encore in an exhibition before leaving for the Olympics. They were the only athletes in the rarefied air of Squaw Valley who did not need supplemental oxygen.

At the October, 1975 meeting of the International Academy of Preventive Medicine one of the exhibitors told me how impressed he was with the marked change in his skiing since he began to take 1,600 IU of vitamin E a day. A year ago he had real difficulty at 8,000 to 10,000 feet, while this year he skied at that altitude for two days without any shortness of breath at all.

In race horses and racing dogs the ability of vitamin E to improve performance has been firmly established, and since they aren't subject to psychological factors, or the powers of suggestion, it is very likely that the changes seen are due to the oxygen-conservation power of vitamin E.

## The New Medical Attitude and a
## Tale of a Voice Restored

The International Academy of Preventive Medicine is one of
the several groups of doctors who are blazing a trail in the
New Medicine. The physicians, surgeons, psychiatrists, and
allied groups take advantage of current medical practices, but
are devoting more and more of their time and interest to preventing disease by all means possible. This involves a thorough
knowledge of the use of megavitamin therapy, and a knowledge
of practical nutrition.

Like all physicians who graduated from medical school
more than three or four years ago, these men had virtually no
formal training in nutrition. Fortunately, they have been able
to enlist the help of many knowledgeable biochemists and
physiologists, and by meeting every six months, learn from
these men and from each other. Roger J. Williams, Emmanuel
Cheraskin, and Linus Pauling are among those who have
assisted in this learning process. Megavitamin experts such as
Drs. Frederick Klenner and Abraham Hoffer have also con-
tributed to this pool of knowledge. In putting it all together,
a sound basis for preventive medicine has emerged.

The result is a whole new world opening up to more and
more physicians—the reassessment of practice methods and
the institution of more complete biological testing. This is
the essence of the New Medicine, the ability to treat, or in
many cases, to prevent a whole spectrum of diseases, an ac-
complishment not possible heretofore.

A young doctor, Murray Susser, from Pittsburgh, Pennsylvania, attending his first meeting with his beautiful young wife,
Kyp, happened to be in line behind my wife and me while
waiting to be seated for breakfast. His wife was obviously
hoarse and I asked about her laryngitis—but I'll let her tell

her own story about the consequences of that chance meeting
and my question about her voice:

I have been studying classical singing since the age of
thirteen. At age twenty-three I began a family and had
four children by age thirty. Gradually, my singing gave
way to refereeing, and at age thirty-three I discovered I
had trouble singing even a few phrases. When I stopped
to think about it, I realized I had laryngitis every week.
Soon people couldn't recognize my voice over the phone.
My husband, a physician, referred me to an ear, nose,
and throat surgeon who found a nodule on each vocal
cord. Surgery to remove them was performed soon after.

I was most anxious to resume my vocal training. I was
frightened about my voice. My teacher insisted I consult
a vocal rehabilitationist in New York before she would
begin lessons with me again. I was examined by an M.D.
whose walls were covered with autographed photos of
Metropolitan Opera stars. He found scar tissue on both
cords and predicted I would never be able to sing again.
He was hopeful that I could progress, with training, to
the point where I could carry on a conversation. There I
was, only able to whisper, sure I would never sing another
aria for an audience, or lullabies for my children.

A month or so later, my husband and I went to Detroit, Michigan to our first meeting of the International
Academy of Preventive Medicine where we shared my
problem with Dr. Wilfrid E. Shute. Dr. Shute asked how
much vitamin E I was taking and recommended I double
the 800 IU I took daily. His intention was to dissolve the
scar tissue on my cords; he asked me to keep in touch.

I went back to Pittsburgh feeling hopeful, still hoarse.
I took the 1,600 IU of vitamin E daily for about three
weeks, and saw no change in my voice. I was terribly
impatient and added another 800 IU on my own. In
about two weeks I found I wasn't clearing my throat
constantly to speak more clearly. I was noticing some
change in ease of speaking. Impatient and anxious I

added still another 800 IU to my daily 2,400 IU of vitamin E.

In another month I hesitatingly called my voice teacher and made an appointment for a vocal analysis. I was speaking in a normal voice by then. We did some easy warming-up exercises and my teacher announced with a smile that my cords sounded healthy!

With carefully graduated singing exercises and daily 3,200 IU of vitamin E, I overcame the crack in my middle range.

Today, at age thirty-seven, I am maintaining on 2,400 IU of vitamin E daily and singing to my children as well as locally. The icing on the cake is the extension of my vocal range three notes and a lyrical quality I never had as a mezzo-soprano. I have been examined by my surgeon twice since my recovery of my voice. He was delighted to tell me that there is no scar tissue on either vocal cord.

It is my joy to share my miracle with you.

Dr. Susser is now a member of the Board of Trustees of the International Academy of Preventive Medicine.

Here is another reference to this gratifying action of vitamin E, as described in a letter from a northwestern state:

. . . I began to use vitamin E after reading your book, *Vitamin E for Ailing and Healthy Hearts* and am now taking 1,000 IU a day. I am simply amazed. I have gained in strength 50 percent. I used to sing but have been losing my voice for the last twenty years and had become resigned to never sing again, and here I am regaining my voice. . . .

# Circulation

*Vitamin E has made some of its most impressive showings in the treatment of circulatory disorders. It really does alleviate phlebitis and intermittent claudication; it does prevent heart attack and improves chances of recovery from one. The evidence is clear on vitamin E's value in these areas, certainly it is better than the more commonly used treatments, but it's an uphill fight to get more doctors to prescribe it. This is particularly puzzling when you consider that many of the treatments routinely prescribed have a poor performance record and some are downright dangerous. The following pages will suggest to you how vitamin E might fit into your circulation picture.*

# Ailments That Commonly Affect the Legs

## Varicose Veins

Knowing the accepted theories of what causes varicose veins, and the accepted forms of treatment—injection, surgical removal, and stripping—we at the Shute Institute anticipated that vitamin E would be no help in treating this ailment. Then our patients who were being treated with vitamin E for various cardiovascular conditions began telling us that their varicose veins were decreasing in size at the same time. Naturally, we began to wonder about possible response.

One day a man showed me a varicose vein inside his right knee the thickness of a finger and about five to six inches long. His main problem was in his heart and this varicosity was coincidental. At a subsequent visit he mentioned that this vein inside his right leg had disappeared. I examined it, and, indeed, it was no longer visible, although I could still feel it under the skin.

My colleagues reported similar stories about their patients. Later, at the International Vitamin E Conference held in Italy, two doctors demonstrated, by microscope, the changes on the walls of varicose veins, brought about by vitamin E. The elastic lamina bands which encircle the vein and which in normal veins appear like a wavy line, show up as an elastic band broken into many tiny pieces in a varicose vein. These doctors showed by microscopic sections that these broken-up pieces would rejoin to show a continuous elastic band. Eventually, as the vein returned to its normal size, the band showed the contracted and wavy appearance characteristic of the elastic layer in the normal vein wall.

I must stress the fact that the improvement in the size and prominence of varicose veins does not always occur, and that their complete disappearance is very rare. The end result depends on many factors, such as the condition of the rest of the veins in the leg, the extent of their involvement, the degree of injury, and many more.

Vitamin E is not given to patients with varicose veins primarily as a means of making the veins disappear. It is given because it relieves the aching and the sense of heaviness and swelling they cause. By decreasing the oxygen need of the tissues and by hastening the opening up of alternate channels, the patient obtains relief.

Surgery performed on varicose veins can usually be avoided. Cases of varicose eczema and varicose ulcers which do not respond to any other treatment will almost always respond to vitamin E, given by mouth and applied locally in ointment.

### Discolored Skin Surrounding Varicose Ulcers

Vitamin E has a favorable effect on the collagenosis (a darkly pigmented area) that develops below the skin around chronic varicose ulcers. Initially, the area shows the evidence of deficient blood supply plus the pigment caused by the escape of red blood cells into the tissues and the cells' consequent breakdown. The hemoglobin from the broken-down red cells, combined with oxygen and probably other gases, forms a pigmented area often extending for several inches around the ulcer. The irritation of these pigments, plus the comparative lack of oxygen, causes an increased formation of scar tissue and that is followed by scar tissue contraction. The result varies, of course, but eventually, in many cases, the leg takes on a characteristic appearance—it looks as if someone had wound a tight pressure bandage around the leg and left it on for a very long time.

One of the first such patients I treated with an adequate amount of vitamin E had experienced severe numbness of the foot below the huge intractable ulcer. As the ulcer healed she noticed a gradual return of sensation in the foot. Now some thirty years after she first started taking vitamin E, she has no residual trace of collagenosis whatsoever, and the pigmentation has all but disappeared. Many such patients have shown lessening of their collagenosis, but just this one had complete recovery from a very profound involvement.

Virtually all patients on vitamin E show a very considerable decrease in pigmentation, beginning around the edge of such pigmented areas. Again, the explanation is the ability of vitamin E to decrease the oxygen need of tissues with an increase in the rate of normal tissue function. Soon the healing mechanisms show an appreciable gain over the disease forces in the involved tissues.

## Intermittent Claudication

The first symptom of intermittent claudication (the result of a hardening of the arteries in the legs) seems simple and rather unimportant. Typically, the patient has been walking for a while—perhaps shopping, out for a stroll, or just back and forth on the job—and suddenly he or she must stop because of a severe cramp in the calf of one leg. Standing still for a short time usually causes the cramp to go away. Then walking can be resumed. In time, the frequency and severity of cramps increase, while the distance that can be covered before the cramps occur, shortens. Eventually, both legs are affected and the patient is no longer ambulatory.

This condition is serious for several other reasons. First, if the patient survives long enough, the ailment will probably progress to gangrene and eventual amputation of one or both legs. Second, the incidence of a heart attack or death from heart failure is greatly increased in these patients.

Dr. Knüt Haeger reported in *Vascular Disease* (5: 199, 1968) and in *Prevention* (March, 1975) on supervised double blind, cross-over trials of vitamin E therapy for these cases. He showed that such patients were not helped significantly by vasodilators, anticoagulants (blood-thinning drugs), or multivitamin capsules that contain no vitamin E. However, they were helped to a significant degree by vitamin E therapy. Dr. Haeger thus confirmed previous work by Dr. A. M. Boyd, professor of surgery at the University of Manchester in England, reported in *Lancet* (2: 132, 1949) and *Journal of Angiology* (14: 198, 1963).

Both Drs. Boyd and Haeger demonstrated that the patients treated with vitamin E survived longer than any other group of claudication patients ever studied. Dr. Boyd used several x rays to show that the calcium, characteristically deposited in the walls of the arteries in advanced arteriosclerotic lesions, was slowly eliminated during the treatment.

However, the most dramatic proof of the power of vitamin E was shown by Haeger's experiment. Among those not given vitamin E who survived (only half as many lived, compared with those in the vitamin E-treated group) there were eleven leg amputations, as against one in those who were given vitamin E. It is likely that the one amputee who was getting vitamin E might well have saved his leg if this experiment had not been a double blind study, where neither the subjects nor the researchers knew who was getting the test substance. Otherwise, he would probably have been placed on an increased—and probably effective—dosage of vitamin E as soon as it was evident that his condition was not improving.

Haeger also demonstrated that the blood supply is, in fact, increased in the legs of intermittent claudication patients treated with vitamin E.

## Buerger's Disease

Buerger's disease is several circulatory problems in one. First, there's inflammation in the lining of the artery of the affected limb, usually followed by hardening of the artery. On top of this there is the tremendous tendency to develop clots. Usually, in the case of the leg, the end result of Buerger's disease is gangrene, progressive gangrene, then amputation.

One of my early Buerger's disease patients came direct from the Mayo Clinic. He had been told that the doctors there were totally unable to prevent gangrene from developing in his great toe. At that time the accepted treatment was to do sympathectomies, that is, cutting the sympathetic nerves to the area in the hope of increasing the blood supply. It did work to some extent, by increasing the superficial blood supply, but it didn't increase the general blood supply. Or if it did, the degree of increase was so small that it really accomplished nothing. (I think that operation has been pretty much abandoned, along with a lot of other surgical procedures that were intended to improve circulation.)

When this patient was first seen, the great toe on one foot was totally dead—black and mummified. The circulation to the rest of the foot and in the leg was critically decreased and amputation was imminent.

Vitamin E was the sole treatment I used on him and circulation greatly improved. The living cells adjacent to the dead cells in the toe were able to slough off the dead cells and the toe eventually dropped off spontaneously (self-amputation). (It is of the utmost importance in such cases that the doctor interfere as little as possible with this process, since anything done may induce fresh damage to the living tissues above the gangrenous area.)

The rest of the foot healed completely and the circulation was so much improved that the man went on with a normal, useful leg that would, otherwise, surely have been taken off above the knee.

The cause of Buerger's disease is unknown and there was no specific treatment for it until we tested the value of vitamin E. In my experience results are universally good.

## Thrombophlebitis

A clot in the bloodstream can occur at any point in the body. Commonly it occurs in the extremities, but it can turn up in the eye, the throat, or anywhere.

It seems to develop most frequently in the legs. I think that's because those vessels are so far from the heart, and they are so long in the leg. A person stands and walks and the result is that the force of gravity can cause more trouble in the legs than in other places where the vessels are shorter and the blood goes through them at a better rate.

Laymen tend to use the terms clot and phlebitis and thrombophlebitis interchangeably. There are very important differences. Phlebitis refers to an inflammation in the vein wall. Phlebothrombosis refers to a clot in the vein. Thrombophlebitis means that there is inflammation of the wall and a clot is present as well.

Clots in the veins of the leg, the most common site of thrombophlebitis, can be very serious for two main reasons. During the acute phase, the whole clot, or part of it, may break loose inside the vein and be carried to and through the heart to be forced into the pulmonary arteries. If the clot is large enough, it may shut off all the blood supply to one or both lungs, or be forced into a branch of the pulmonary artery and shut off the blood supply to an area of the lung. This condition, called pulmonary embolism, carries a death rate of 50 percent.

The second serious consequence of thrombophlebitis concerns the development of the clot in the veins with progressive fibrosis which eventually leads to the vein's being obstructed at that point. When damage to a large vein is sufficiently extensive, the return blood flow decreases. Swelling and a sense of heaviness and aching in the leg result, and, in some cases where there is minor injury, chronic varicose ulcers develop.

Phlebitis has a habit of recurring, and each recurrence takes its toll of available venous drainage, leading to an increase of signs and symptoms and the increased danger of ulceration.

Vitamin E, properly used, will dissolve the fresh clot without increasing the danger of embolism. It does this in dramatic fashion, usually in a matter of hours or days, with no residual damage to the return of blood from the leg. However, the tendency to recurrence of phlebitis must be controlled by a maintenance dose of vitamin E for the rest of the patient's life.

The response vitamin E brings in treating chronic phlebitis —the condition which arises in many of those who have already suffered an acute attack—is variable. The treatment is usually very much worthwhile, but may take several weeks to show its value in any given case.

Some years after we'd been using vitamin E to treat thrombophlebitis, my brother Evan, who is an obstetrician and gynecologist, had a patient with a D & C in the hospital. On the day he went in to discharge her, he discovered that she had developed a tremendous thrombophlebitis in her thigh. Here was a chance to show other doctors what vitamin E could do, he thought.

It was winter and the doctors entered that hospital through a cloakroom where they left their overcoats and overshoes. They passed by a bulletin board there where any information of interest to doctors was posted. On this bulletin board my brother put a sign saying "Mrs. Jones in room 000 had a D & C three days ago. I came in to discharge her today and she has a tremendous thrombophlebitis in her thigh, very visible and palpable. I've put her on 800 units of vitamin E and the thrombophlebitis will be gone in three days. This lady has given permission to any doctor to come and speak with her and examine her as the vitamin E treatment goes on. I repeat: the thrombophlebitis will be gone in three days, so I suggest that you go today."

The next day he posted another note saying, "The thrombophlebitis is half gone, but the lady is still in the hospital and if you want to see her please see her today."

On the third day he announced, "There is no evidence that this patient ever had a thrombophlebitis, but she will be in the hospital for another day or two. If you want to talk with her about her experience with vitamin E, please visit her."

It is interesting that only two doctors from that whole staff ever visited that patient. Even they visited by coincidence. Both of them happened to be passing by in the hall when my brother was coming out of the room. He grabbed them and said "You've talked a lot about the value of vitamin E, now come and see for yourselves what it does."

Remember, we're discussing a cure for a major problem in surgery and medicine. Still my brother couldn't arouse any interest in it among the doctors in a major hospital.

A remarkable case involved a redheaded Irish woman. (For some reason, redheads are more likely to develop rheumatic heart disease or rheumatic fever than blonds, and blonds more likely than brunettes. I was taught that in medical school but I found it hard to believe until my experience proved it to be true.) This redheaded woman developed a very large clot in the varicose veins in her thigh. She had been Evan's obstetrical patient and he prescribed 600 IU of vitamin E daily. The clot cleared up completely as far as anybody could tell within three and a half days. At her next pregnancy she developed thrombophlebitis in the same leg between the knee and the ankle and, again, with vitamin E, this cleared up in four and a half days.

At every subsequent pregnancy (and this woman got pregnant once a year for the next five years), she developed phlebitis in that leg but on each occasion she put herself on vitamin E. She didn't even bother telling Evan until her next visit when she would report another phlebitis which had cleared up on vitamin E. She should have been on a maintenance dose, but wouldn't agree to it.

Let me tell you about a nurse I treated, very obese, about sixty years old, who developed this tremendous phlebitis. The case was complicated by her suffering from both hypertension and rheumatic heart disease. Either of these complications requires careful dosage with vitamin E. Yet phlebitis calls for large dosages of E in a hurry. This was a true dilemma.

I talked to the patient about it. I told her I planned to put her on 800 IU of vitamin E per day, and that such a dosage would ordinarily be too big for anyone who had rheumatic damage to her heart along with high blood pressure. I predicted that the phlebitis would be nearly gone in ten days but she would start to have shortness of breath, pounding of the heart, and general distress at about that time.

I saw her then in ten days and she had developed the pounding and shortness of breath I predicted, and the phlebitis had almost gone. It had been there for some weeks before I saw her, so it wasn't as simple as an acute one which can be cleared in three days. I stopped her vitamin E for a day and a half, then cut her down to a small dose and maintained her on that for about a week. Then I put her back to 800 IU knowing that once more she would get into trouble in ten days. Well, she did. But by this time the phlebitis had cleared up completely.

Recently, I was prevailed upon to see one of my fellow villagers in Florida, a woman who was seriously ill with thrombophlebitis. She had gone to her doctor who prescribed anti-coagulants and put her in the hospital. She had been in and out of the hospital twice and, over the course of months, saw no results whatsoever. Her legs were tremendously swollen. When I went to see her she was sitting in a chair with the most affected leg elevated and wrapped. The entire leg was so swollen and had so much phlebitis that it obviously involved the veins in her pelvis too.

I put her on 1,600 IU of vitamin E a day. Three weeks after she went on the treatment the leg was nearly normal and the woman was driving her own car and doing her own shopping. When I saw her she was at a bridge party, looking fine, pain-free.

Of course, one of the most widely reported cases of phlebitis was the one suffered by the former president, Richard M. Nixon. There's no way of my knowing what caused his problem. I don't know if he had any specific injury to his leg or if the psychological tension he was under was affecting his circulatory apparatus, or whether the phlebitis was just spontaneous

—as it can be. I do know that if I had seen Mr. Nixon when he first developed the thrombophlebitis I could have cleared it up in three days or less, by giving him 800 to 1,600 IU of vitamin E daily. My brother and I have done this hundreds of times in treating phlebitis. It's hard for me to believe that none of the important doctors in attendance knew enough to treat ex-President Nixon with vitamin E.

Now you can never recover completely from phlebitis and the disease does have a tendency to repeat when patients are treated in the orthodox manner. So it is most likely that Mr. Nixon will have another thrombophlebitis, and this time it could well be fatal. On the other hand, if Mr. Nixon were on a maintenance dosage of vitamin E of 800 IU daily, a recurrence would be highly unlikely, if not impossible. He could have been treated successfully in the first place, with no danger of the pulmonary embolism that developed. He would have had a speedy, uneventful cure in three or four days. No doubt about it, no argument.

# Heart Disease

## Congenital Heart Problems

All patients with congenital heart disease that can be cured or improved by surgery should have the surgery. In a few conditions a successful operation results in normalcy. In others, there is worthwhile improvement, even though the patient may not obtain completely normal function.

Vitamin E therapy has a very important role in all cases of congenital heart disease. Because of its power to reduce the oxygen need of all tissues, including tissues of the heart muscle itself, vitamin E is essential in the preoperative preparation of the patient as well as in the postoperative period. Further, vitamin E has the ability to prevent unnecessary and dangerous intravascular clotting, *safely*. At the same time, it does not interfere with normal healing. In fact, it speeds up the normal healing process in such cases.

However, in those patients where no surgical procedure is possible, vitamin E is absolutely essential. A proportion of such patients, the so-called "blue babies," for example, show *cyanosis* (a blue coloring of the skin) of varying degrees. Many show the effects of generalized *anoxia* (lack of oxygen) of tissues and are subject to frequent upper respiratory infections in addition to decreased exercise tolerance. Many patients tend to "squat" when they are short of breath, since in this position their thighs support their abdominal muscles, which are used as accessory muscles to help their breathing.

Here visual proof of the efficacy of vitamin E therapy is obvious. In almost every case the cyanosis decreases in response to vitamin E, occasionally it disappears entirely, although it may show up a little during strenuous physical activity. The child who was purple becomes blue, the child who was blue is less so, or even normal in coloring. The habit of squatting is reduced or eliminated, and resistance to upper respiratory tract infections is increased.

In these congenital heart cases, the decrease in cyanosis is the visible evidence of improved tissue oxygenation and consequent improvement in tissue function throughout the body.

This may be the place to point out that virtually all patients on vitamin E treatment experience another visible proof of improved tissue function: fingernails and toenails grow noticeably faster. Hair grows faster, too, but alas, not thicker, nor any more numerous!

Finally, there is the question of survival. Many patients with congenital heart disease die prematurely from intercurrent infections or from the results of a life with oxygen-poor organs and tissues. Most of the blue baby type develop *polycythemia* (an excess of red blood cells) and have, therefore, an increased incidence of thrombosis affecting the vessels of the brain, especially when dehydration from any cause occurs. Congenital heart disease patients have an increased susceptibility to bacterial *endocarditis* (inflammation of the inner wall of the heart), and brain abscesses also tend to occur more frequently in this type of patient.

The prognosis in cases of congenital heart disease is generally poor. Many die in childhood or in their twenties. In fact, most colleges and universities are reluctant to accept them as students.

I had experience with such a case some years ago. I had treated this boy since he was ten years of age and had great difficulty persuading a mid-western university to accept him as a student. He graduated with high honors and now teaches school, including some night classes and summer school. He supervises playground activities, has obtained his Ph.D. in education, and runs an arts and crafts shop as a sideline to all this. He is now thirty-five years old and physically well, an outstanding citizen in his mid-western town.

Without vitamin E, this man would almost certainly be long since dead. Of course, he knows this. All his other doctors had told his family he had a short life expectancy before he came to me as a last resort.

**My Own Problem**    I myself was born with a congenital heart problem, a defective aortic valve. My first symptoms began when I was around twelve years of age, when I had sensations of weakness, and again about twenty years ago when I had an episode during which I had serious heart symptoms. In spite of this I was an intercollegiate champion wrestler, which is obviously a very energetic occupation. Also, for years I have shown my own Doberman pinschers, which are big dogs. When you get into a ring with a judge who likes to run you around to evaluate gait, you go around the ring three or four times very often at a fairly rapid pace. I had no problems in doing this. I also played golf without any problem for years.

Suddenly one day at a dog show, when I was about sixty-five years old, I had a near-fainting episode. After that my ability to walk and to engage in vigorous activities deteriorated. I had several blackouts in which I collapsed completely and was unconscious for as long as an hour. The last time this happened my heart stopped beating and my son-in-law had to pound me on the chest to get it started again.

Let me explain the cause of my condition. The aortic valve has three cusps but mine only had two. In such cases, over the years, the edges of the valve tend to unite with scar tissue and the valve opening gets steadily smaller, a situation which doesn't happen with the three cusp valves. So all people with this congenital disease gradually get into trouble, and nearly always it happens much earlier than it did in my case. I've taken 1,600 IU of vitamin E a day for twenty years or more. I believe that is why I was able to postpone major surgery for so long.

I have a great friend who ran into the same trouble with blackouts when he was in his forties. Other members of his family had died unexpectedly of an unexplained cardiac condition. He had the living members of his family checked and a congenital bicuspid aortic valve was found in four or five of them. All of them have now been operated on.

Anybody who has read my books will know I have always insisted that any patient of mine suffering from a congenital heart disease must submit to surgery if the condition is operable. I most certainly would advise anybody with a bicuspid congenital valve to be operated on. In my case I postponed the surgery too long, and it became a desperate situation that resulted in a four-month hospital stay for me *before* I could be operated on. But the results have been fantastically good. I'm better than I've been for ten years. I can do almost anything I ever did before. I want to emphasize that this type of corrective operation has nothing to do with by-pass surgery at all, a measure to which I am opposed.

### Rheumatic Fever and Chronic Rheumatic Heart Disease

Rheumatic fever is related to an infection of tonsils or lymph glands in the nose and throat area. Adequate treatment of the initial infection (hemolytic streptococcus Group A) with antibiotics prevents the disease, otherwise rheumatic fever can develop some seven to ten days later. At that point antibiotics are useless. Salicylates and steroids might ease the symptoms, but they can't change the course of the disease.

Unfortunately, 80 percent of those who contract acute rheumatic fever develop rheumatic heart disease. Chronic rheumatic heart disease still accounts for 30 percent of crippled hearts and about 50 percent of heart disease deaths that occur before the age of thirty.

When vitamin E is used as part of the treatment in acute cases, all signs and symptoms of the disease disappear within two to four days, without after-effects.

The early signs of chronic rheumatic fever—shortness of breath, pounding of the heart, and swelling of liver or extremities or both—progress until the patient literally drowns in his own juices. About 10 percent of the victims die short of their normal life expectancy due to thrombosis or infarction.

Most chronic rheumatic fever victims can be helped; some can even be returned to normal activity with a total disappearance of symptoms and their lives prolonged for years. The first patients of this type treated by me with vitamin E are still doing very well twenty-eight years later.

However, anyone treating such a patient with vitamin E must observe detailed precautions exactly. This is because, in a large proportion of such patients, the damage to one side of the heart is greater than to the other side, and the therapeutic dose to which the patient will eventually respond helps the good side faster than the poor side. This throws the heart out of balance if it is on the verge of such trouble or increases any imbalance that has already begun to show. If a small dosage, too small to cause demonstrable improvement, is given initially, then slowly increased, it will permit the more damaged side to improve and catch up to the better side, restoring the heart's former presymptom balance. Then the dosage level can be safely increased with the whole heart improving while maintaining balance.

To repeat: we start all *acute* cases of rheumatic fever on 800 IU of vitamin E or more a day—but *chronic* cases are started on 90 IU a day for the first month, 120 IU for the second month, and 150 IU thereafter. For real worthwhile improvement, 150 IU of vitamin E may be sufficient; some patients cannot tolerate more and do not need more.

This procedure is so safe and so effective in chronic rheumatic heart disease patients in the early stages of symptomatology, that I have successfully treated such cases over the telephone, restoring their clinical condition in three and a half months to what it was ten years previously.

Of course, many patients with symptoms that range from mild to most severe have suffered damage on both sides of the heart, and such patients respond within a few days to the therapeutic dose. However, it is impossible to predict which ones will and which ones will not. That is why we urge careful adherence to the initial small-dose schedule. This is the most important situation in which fitting the dose of vitamin E to the patient's requirements must be remembered.

Recognizing the functions of vitamin E and its compatabilities with other vitamins and drugs and foods is, of course, of the essence. Specific cases, where these rules have been broken successfully in critical conditions, are many. One of the most interesting has come to my attention by mail and I must reproduce this letter from Mrs. B—— W—— (written March 15, 1976) in detail:

In 1942, while serving in the Armed Forces, my husband had a severe strep infection. As a result he de-

veloped acute rheumatic fever. After many months in a
Naval Hospital he was given a medical discharge because
of the severe heart damage that resulted.

After our marriage in 1944 my husband (who will be
referred to from now on as Bill) spent almost as much
time in the V.A. Hospital as he spent at home. The
doctors prescribed digitalis and 400,000 mgs. of penicillin
as a prophylaxis against further strep infection. Even on
this medication and a completely "salt-free" diet he still
had symptoms such as edema, shortness of breath without exertion, and when he was taken to the hospital for
an emergency appendectomy in 1955, he was in heart
failure.

Because of the time required for treatment in a V.A.
hospital he became the patient of a local doctor who kept
him on the medication and added a diuretic.

He worked as much as possible but continued to spend
much time in the hospital until, after an annual check-up
in 1967, our local doctor suggested that he enter the
University Hospital where the doctors there work along
with the V.A. Hospital. He felt he should have surgery to
replace the mitral valve because the mitral stenosis had
become so severe.

Bill underwent all of the examinations for Open Heart
Surgery including the catheter that almost cost him his
life at the time.

Even though surgery was scheduled I wasn't ready to
take on the task of raising our children alone so I suggested we try something our son had been studying about
as a result of his interest in weight lifting—namely vitamin E. I had read Dr. Shute's book on vitamin E, Adelle
Davis' book "Let's Get Well" and also much literature in
other books including *Prevention* magazine.

One thing I missed in all of the reading was the warning about small doses for chronic rheumatic heart disease.
I started with a dosage of 500 IU and in a month put him
up to 700 IU. Even though he was doing miraculously
on 700 IU I cut back on the dosage when I finally read

of the warning but I raised it to 700 IU again within two weeks because he seemed much better at that level.

As usual I made the annual check-up appointments for a cardiac work-up because I was fearful of being responsible if I didn't do all I could medically. When he was examined by the doctor he didn't ask any questions about the "surgery" that Bill *didn't* have but he told him to continue along with the medication he was on. At this point he was told that he was on vitamin E plus the other vitamins and he said Bill was doing fine so continue. This was the first time since 1942 he hadn't been on any medication and the first time he had been able to work regularly.

It has been nine years since Bill first started taking vitamin E and in that length of time he has missed only ten or twelve days work—none of these because of his heart.

All of this seemed like a miracle and I was completely shaken when he developed strange sores on his toes and the toes become so swollen it was extremely painful to walk.

After a trip to our family physician I was really upset when he said his problem was vascular and sent him to a surgeon. After a test the doctor diagnosed Bill's problem as Raynauds phenomenon with gangrene. He suggested a lumbar sympathectomy to try and cause more circulation in his feet—otherwise, he said, he would lose his toes—bit by bit, because of the gangrene.

When this schedule of surgery was set for April 30, 1975, again I was repulsed by the thought so again I started reading but found nothing until our son ordered a book *Alpha Tocopherol in Cardiovascular Disease* by Dr. W. E. Shute. It was printed on demand by University Microfilms, a Xerox company in Michigan. This book seemed to be written about Bill but again the warning loomed up because of the rheumatic heart. In desperation I began to locate Dr. Shute and after many phone calls found where he had been in California. Since

Dr. Shute was not at the institute in California, I talked to Dr. Rudolph Alsleben. I explained the situation briefly and explained about the current crisis, Dr. Alsleben suggested 3,000 IU of vitamin E even though Bill has a damaged heart. He explained that since his heart had successfully tolerated 700 IU of vitamin E for nine years the larger amount would not be harmful to him.

Again—feeling responsible for a life—I raised the vitamin E dosage more slowly. I put Bill on 1,600 IU as soon as I talked with Dr. Alsleben and have now raised it to 2,400 IU. Two weeks after he started on 1,600 IU vitamin E, the only sign of an abnormal condition on his feet was a tiny white piece of skin that was in the place of the large open sore, and the toes were normal in size instead of extremely swollen as before. I'm sure the surgeon that was to operate is wondering where my husband is, the person reading this that has never heard of such a 'miracle' is wondering if it is a 'fairy-tale' but the proof is in seeing the end results.

I imagine I should explain why I am writing this. Just recently I finished reading Dr. W. E. Shute's book . . . *Complete, Updated Vitamin E Book* and once again there appeared in print the warning about dosage of vitamin E and rheumatic heart disease. I became so frustrated that once again I began a search for Dr. Shute and finally succeeded in reaching him.

After one more explanation about our situation Dr. Shute asked that I send an account of our success with vitamin E. I am so thankful for vitamin E. Because of it I've had my husband thirty-two years instead of being a widow for many years.

Two more cases which illustrate the importance of tailoring the dose to the type of pathological process and to the individual's need, come to mind.

The first concerns one of the young nurses working at the Shute Institute in London, Ontario. She had no symptoms related to heart disease although she had a questionable history of rheumatic fever as a child. No one who worked at the institute could fail to be impressed with the response of the patients there, especially the nurses and the doctors. So this nurse began to take vitamin E. After about ten days she noticed some pounding of her heart—a symptom she had not had before. On examination, it was obvious that she had some rheumatic heart damage and she was then placed on the slow, small dosage vitamin E routine.

Four years later, when she was walking downtown a big dog came running along the sidewalk and knocked her into the street, ruining her stockings and skinning her knees. Hours later when she returned home, she washed the dirt off her knees and thought no more of it.

After a few days this young woman began to experience bizarre symptoms which she did not at first relate to her skinned knees. Then she developed some stiffness of the jaw, a stiff neck, and then spasms with extreme retraction of her head and rigidity in her back. A diagnosis of tetanus was made and she was given tetanus antitoxin in the usual dosage. Because most of the tetanus toxin is set in the body at this stage and because of the muscle spasms, but particularly to increase the oxidative functions of the affected central nervous system cells, she was given 1,600 IU of vitamin E a day, more than five times the amount she had been able to tolerate before the tetanus infection. Her recovery was rapid and complete.

Certainly this woman had reached an extremely serious stage of the disease before treatment began. We all were sure that the vitamin E was most effective and was responsible for the rapidity and completeness of her recovery. We felt that it speeded up the release of the set toxins and their excretion, since the antitoxin only neutralizes the toxins produced by the tetanus organism that have not yet become set.

I mention this case because we have now seen several patients who could not tolerate over 300 IU of vitamin E a day because of severe rheumatic heart disease damage, yet they were able to tolerate it when an emergency arose which required a dosage in the range of 1,600 IU at least long enough to allow recovery from the emergency.

Another example concerns a doctor who tried to take vitamin E but said that he could not tolerate it. He joined the Canadian army but was not allowed to go overseas because of a murmur in his heart and a suspicion of chronic rheumatic heart disease. He had tried vitamin E but stopped because it caused his heart to pound and gave him a little shortness of breath. However, by pulling strings in Ottawa he did go overseas and served in England for the rest of World War II.

Years later, it was decided that this doctor's gallbladder must be removed and he telephoned me to see what dosage of vitamin E he should take to prepare for the surgery. This was a difficult situation. I wanted to tell him to avoid the operation since I knew the risk heart patients face in surgery. But it was too late for that. He was scheduled for the operation the day after he telephoned me. There really wasn't time for the vitamin E to protect him, especially since he couldn't take any vitamin E by mouth the day of the operation. Furthermore, he was a doctor and he was under the care of a surgeon; it was not my place to interfere.

I was not surprised when I received a telephone call from the patient's wife a couple of days after the operation saying he had developed phlebitis. A clot had broken loose and gone to his lungs and he was critically ill. Of course there was but one answer—massive vitamin E. Fortunately, the patient responded rapidly and was himself operating in that same hospital ten days later. Here was another case where the patient was able to tolerate a large dose during the emergency and this patient has been on a large dose ever since.

The first five of our patients with chronic rheumatic heart disease amazed me with their rapid and complete clinical recovery on 300 to 600 IU of vitamin E. For example, although the heart of one patient was grossly enlarged and he was in early congestive failure when we began to treat him, he was symptom-free in four days, and back to work in a week. However, after two or three unfortunate episodes involving other patients whose cases appeared to be quite similar to this man's, we learned to be cautious in our treatment of patients with chronic rheumatic heart disease.

Most of these patients, when given large doses of vitamin E, show rapid marked improvement in four or five days; but they are not as well in ten days. In three or four weeks they are in serious trouble, worse than they were before vitamin E treatment. Fortunately, when vitamin E is withdrawn, the excess is rapidly excreted and no real harm is done.

It is unfortunate that we do not have any way of telling beforehand how an individual suffering from chronic rheumatic heart disease will react to various dosages of vitamin E. In general, the patient who responds too quickly and too well in three to six days is probably on too large a dose and the slow, small dosage regime will have to be used.

## Myocardial Infarction or "Heart Attack"

When I was graduated from medical school in 1933, myo-cardial infarction or "heart attack" was a relatively rare disease of old men. Today it is a leading cause of death. It occurs when the blood supply to an area of the heart is decreased to a point where the muscle fibers of the heart die. If the affected area is big enough, the patient dies suddenly. Some victims live for a short time after an attack, and some—depending on many factors—survive for years, apparently recovered.

Ordinarily, heart attack victims have one chance in three of living long enough to have treatment at all. (Sixty-five percent die suddenly or are dead on arrival at the hospital.) The old statistics said that 50 percent of those who survived were dead at the end of a year and that 15 percent survived five years. Naturally, the American Heart Association and the cardiologists play down the dangers of a coronary thrombosis and the grim expectations after survival of the attack. However, the fact is that with the treatment commonly used, most of these patients, or at least a large number of them, have a second, and if they survive that, a third attack, and die early.

I know it sounds surprising, but forty-five years ago, the doctors who taught me cardiology were not kept sufficiently busy with any type of heart patients to warrant exclusive attention to this phase of medicine. Treating heart disease was just a small but important part of their medical practice.

Today the number of cardiologists is legion. And the sad thing is that today this increasing army of specialists is needed. The obvious corollary is that the cardiologists haven't been able to stem the tide of this killer. Indeed, I believe just about everything they have done is wrong.

I'll name two of the many errors I see:

First, the almost immediate acceptance of anticoagulants (blood thinners), and the extensive use of them for twelve years before it became obvious that the anticoagulants neither saved human lives nor prevented future attacks. The *Journal of the American Medical Association* (August 3, 1970) carried an editorial titled "An Exercise in Futility" that backs up my point. And many more medical journals, including the *Canadian Medical Association Journal* way back in 1960, have expressed skepticism about these drugs.

Many doctors have abandoned the use of the so-called "blood thinners." However, those doctors who feel that one must appear to be doing something, continue to prescribe these useless, dangerous drugs. That is why they continue to appear in the pharmacy of nearly every hospital in Canada and the United States.

Second, the adoption and promotion of the low cholesterol diet. This theory originated in 1850 and was soon abandoned. It was revived by Ancel Keys who related the growing epidemic of heart attack, and blood vessel narrowing in general, to the increased use of animal fats. The Ancel Keys theory was based on three major fallacies. One, that there has been a significant increase in the use of animal fats in the American diet, when there really has not. Two, that the incidence of coronary thrombosis or myocardial infarction, which has increased almost continuously since it was first discovered in 1912, is directly related to the incidence of coronary artery arteriosclerosis. Actually, the incidence of coronary artery arteriosclerosis has not increased, at least during this century (Morris, J.N., *Lancet,* 1.69,1951 and Glatzel, H., *Arztliche Praxis,* November, 1971). Three, that there is a relationship between arteriosclerosis and thrombosis in a vessel, when, in fact, there is no such relationship.

The Glatzel paper shows that the wide acceptance and extensive use of low cholesterol diets containing an increased proportion of polyunsaturated fats and a decreased proportion of animal fats, not only hasn't decreased the incidence of heart attack, but indeed has had the exact opposite effect. The gradual increase in the incidence of myocardial infarction (heart attacks) suddenly accelerated, actually began to increase precipitously. And this rise continued until very recently when, in my opinion, the effect of the public's increased use of megavitamin E led to a significant decrease (10,000 fewer deaths in 1975 than expected among middle-aged men).

I believe the high-powered advertising on TV and radio of margarines containing a high proportion of polyunsaturated fats, and their wide acceptance and use, is one of the greatest catastrophes to befall the American public in this century.

The polyunsaturated fats use up vitamin E. Anybody on a diet high in these fats should increase his intake of vitamin E. It has been suggested by one California researcher, Dr. Daniel B. Menzel, that every American must have a minimum of 200 units of vitamin E per day. Dr. M. K. Horwitt, who was our number one antagonist, and who criticized my brother for suggesting vitamin E treatment after the Japanese vitamin E conference, has now come around to admitting that vitamin E is a potent antithrombic agent. He says that the Recommended Daily Allowance must be reviewed and probably increased.

Virtually all cardiologists, in fact most doctors, advise their patients to avoid what have become known as "the risk factors," one of which is animal fats. I will merely quote Dr. Elliot Corday on this subject in order to demonstrate how at least one doctor at the policy-making level views the true value of such advice:

> "As a practitioner, I must follow the principles followed in everyday practice. But as a researcher and a member of the heart advisory council (The National Heart Advisory Council), I see the facts from all the reports and I see that we are on the wrong track. Let's tell our patients that we believe this advice should be followed but that we have no real proof that eliminating the risk factors will prevent progression of the disease."

The orthodox treatment of myocardial infarction is clearly

unsatisfactory and has remained so for the last forty years, except for instituting early ambulation, and, in some quarters, the armchair treatment proposed by Samuel Levine in 1951.

Is it any wonder that cardiologists welcomed the number of newer surgical procedures designed to overcome the effects of heart attacks in those patients who survived long enough to leave the hospital?

Among the most popular of these operations is so-called bypass surgery, and it has been urged upon countless patients. In fact, several hundred thousand of these bypasses have been done. And they have been done in spite of statements by many eminent physicians that the operation has shown no evidence of value, either in alleviating symptoms or prolonging life.

Statistically speaking, one patient out of every five who have the operation has a heart attack on the table. Of those who survive, 18 percent have an attack within one year.

By the end of one year, 22 percent of the veins used to bypass the pathological area in the artery are occluded—not just narrowed, but completely closed.

Fifty percent of those who had symptoms before the operation are worse after having it.

It is claimed that 60 percent of those operated on have relief from angina. But then 60 percent to 70 percent also are relieved of pain by a sham operation in which the skin is cut and sewn up again without completing the operation. Then, too, 60 percent of patients lose their pain with a placebo—a sugar pill.

Dr. R. S. Ross, of the Cardiovascular Disease Division of the Department of Medicine, Johns Hopkins Hospital, suggests that the reason the operation relieves the patient's pain is not because it increases the blood supply to the ischemic area in the heart, but because this area dies and is no longer able to initiate pain. In his report, "Ischemic Heart Disease: An Overview" (which appeared in the *American Journal of Cardiology,* 36: 496-505, October, 1975), Dr. Ross further suggests that the disturbance, due to the operation, of the tiny nerves supplying the outer surface of the involved artery may

also play a significant role in reducing the symptoms. He
continues, "Unfortunately, surgery has not been documented
to improve ventricular function nor prolong the natural history
of patients with ischemic disease." In other words, Dr. Ross
sees no apparent relationship between the operation and
avoiding future heart attack or improving life expectancy.

Nevertheless, cardiologists continue to refer patients for this
surgery, and surgeons continue to operate.

The cardiologist can diagnose the cause of disease in a high
proportion of his heart patients, but the heart surgeon quite
often finds a different cause when he opens the patient's heart.
The cardiologist can treat symptoms and severe complications
reasonably well, but he cannot improve the basic health of a
single heart unless he knows how to use vitamin E therapy
correctly. Vitamin E is remarkably useful in treating all kinds
of coronary artery disease. I've seen it work near miracles.

Here is one such case.

For years one of my hobbies has been the breeding, showing, and judging of purebred dogs, and many years ago I
bought two pups from people who now live in Carmel Valley,
California. The wife developed a case of coronary occlusion
(a myocardial infarction) due to obstruction in one of the
coronary arteries and was treated at a very famous medical
clinic in California. There she was put on a cholesterol-free
diet and given all sorts of medicines. None of the treatment
was the least bit effective. Finally the couple decided to come
up to see me in Canada, at the Shute Institute.

When they arrived the poor woman couldn't walk across the
room without experiencing severe chest pains. She had been
in the hospital twice before with heart failure, once soon after
the attack and once just before she became my patient. At
that point, if she had continued the treatment she was on, I
truly believe her chances of surviving a year were less than 50
percent, and chances of surviving two years were nil.

We put her on a vitamin E regimen (this was at least
twenty-five years ago). I saw her at her home recently. She
is now in her seventies and wonderfully well. She is very
active—even judges dogs, a very demanding hobby. She

swims every day (they have their own swimming pool) and she has no symptoms whatsoever.

This patient and her husband celebrated their fiftieth wedding anniversary in September, 1977. The family asked that I be sure to attend.

Vitamin E decreases the heart muscle's need for oxygen prophylactically and therapeutically. After all, it is the substance that has been present in the human bloodstream since the first man, functioning to prevent clots in blood vessels, including, of course, the coronary arteries.

Vitamin E acts in several ways to benefit the victim of a heart attack. Given at the very first moment possible after the attack, it will minimize the extent of the damage to the muscle, by decreasing the affected area's need for oxygen. It may greatly limit the area involved. Later, by speeding up the opening of collateral circulation and by decreasing the oxygen need of the muscle surrounding the affected area, it will support this zone and prevent any extension of the infarct.

Further, vitamin E will prevent contraction of the scar tissue which replaces the area of heart muscle lost when its blood supply is cut off. Usually, this scar tissue contraction squeezes out the capillaries in the area involved. It is believed that the contracted scar tissue without blood supply acts as a foreign body and may therefore initiate ventricular fibrillation and sudden death. Maintaining the blood supply avoids this. Because the scar tissue doesn't contract, due to the use of vitamin E, the blood supply in the area is maintained.

Even if the patient is not fortunate enough to have vitamin E from the onset of his infarction, results of megavitamin E therapy can still be of life-saving value. Of course, in case of delay, the extent of infarction will be greater. Also, contraction of the scar tissue may be advanced and may have already squeezed out the blood vessels supplying it.

However, vitamin E makes the rest of the heart muscle function better due to the decrease of oxygen need. Collateral blood supply increases and the chance for clots in major and minor vessels is minimized. So the whole heart is helped and, of great importance, the chance of a recurrence is greatly lessened.

### The "Angina" that Can Be Cured with Ointment

Recently I had a telephone call from a man who, as a hospital administrator, has had intimate contact with the medical profession and its individual members for over twenty-five years. In the past this man occasionally suffered from angina pectoris on exertion. For some years he was free of it, then he experienced a return of that type of severe chest pain. This time the cardiologists said it was *status anginosus,* a diagnosis indicating severe, prolonged, repeated attacks of chest pain due to deficient blood supply to an extensive area of heart muscle. This man was telephoning to ask if I knew of a doctor in his area using intravenous chelation. He hoped that such treatment would remove any calcium deposited in the walls of his coronary arteries, allowing for increased blood supply to the oxygen-starved heart muscle.

On questioning him it was immediately apparent that his symptoms were just not due to his heart. I have taken care of over 35,000 cardiovascular patients and I have never seen a case of *status anginosus.* What this man had was intercostal neuralgia or intercostal neuritis or radiculitis—it has a variety of names—a well-authenticated entity, almost totally ignored by the profession. It is due to nerve root irritation and has definite, typical, easily elicited signs and symptoms.

Angina pectoris, literally "pain of the chest," is caused by exercise or excitement only when due to heart disease. It must be induced by a heart trying to increase its output on the demand of exertion or excitement. This other condition occurs when the patient is at rest, in a chair, or in bed, or standing, and is induced by movement of the chest wall or a twist in the upper spine. It is usually relieved by a stretching of the arms or a change in position, and is always accompanied by a definite tenderness between the ribs on pressure. This tenderness leads to a corresponding area at the spine.

The answer to this problem can be very simple. First locate the tender area between a pair of ribs and follow it around to the specific area beside the spine where pressure will always elicit pain. Then rub vitamin E ointment into that area each evening for ten minutes, gently, and follow this with heat for ten minutes, and presto, the pain is gone in one to three nights of treatment.

This is what happened in my caller's case: relief of *"status anginosus,"* no heart operation, and no chelation necessary because it had nothing to do with the heart.

Another case of *"status anginosus"* cured by this simple procedure comes to mind. One of my brother Evan's gynecological patients was hospitalized for rest treatment for this condition. Her daughter, also a patient of Evan's, insisted on a consultation with the internist who had made the diagnosis and who had insisted on hospitalization. It was immediately evident to Evan that what she had was this rib syndrome or intercostal neuralgia and one treatment with vitamin E ointment and heat cured her *"status anginosus."* She was discharged symptom-free.

A further interesting aspect of this condition is that it is commonly in the chest, usually on the left side of right-handed patients to a point where if a patient complains of it on the right side you can bet he is left-handed and be right nine times out of ten.

The same symptoms of pain in a localized area can occur anywhere along one side of the body or the other, and when it is lower in the chest can give symptoms which are very frequently diagnosed incorrectly as being due to peptic ulcer, gallbladder disease, even kidney pathology, and the surgeons are often surprised when an operation shows no abnormalities in this direction.

Vitamin E ointment helps in this condition because, as shown by J. F. Burgess and J. E. Pritchard in the *Canadian Medical Association Journal* (59:242, 1948), vitamin E penetrates the skin quickly. This was demonstrated by staining techniques showing E to be present at the periosteum of bone within a short time of exterior application. It penetrates right to the nerve root.

# Other Major Disorders

*Among other major disorders, vitamin E's effect on diabetes is surely the most dramatic. It allows for a reduction in regular insulin dosage and has effectively reversed arterial changes leading to impaired vision and to gangrene. Acute glomerulonephritis responds immediately if vitamin E is given at the onset. The vitamin's action on ailments such as arthritis and multiple sclerosis is less defined, but the indications of a beneficial effect are, I think, persuasive.*

## Diabetes Mellitus

The great need for effective therapy in the treatment of diabetes is obvious as witness this press release dated December 1975:

Washington. A study group recommended yesterday that the government triple its research on diabetes, saying the disease affects 10 million Americans and is the nation's third ranking killer. Only heart disease and cancer, in that order, take more lives, the National Commission on Diabetes said in its first report to Congress.

Laymen and doctors alike need to remember that the great discovery of insulin did nothing to decrease the incidence of diabetes mellitus. It prolongs the lives of many diabetics but does not prevent the degenerative changes in the walls of the arteries.

Regardless of how well a diabetic's blood sugar is controlled, regardless of whether the diabetes is mild, moderate, or severe, all females and most males develop unusually rapid and severe hardening of the arteries, chiefly involving the vessels of the eyes, brain, kidneys, or extremities, or a combination of these.

By decreasing the need for more oxygen, preventing clotting in vessels, and opening up collateral circulation, the effects of the diabetic arterial changes can be halted and reversed even when the condition is severe. I mean severe even to the point where, for example, gangrene of the toes has developed. Very rarely is any additional tissue lost after vitamin E therapy is initiated. Therefore, amputation of the involved limb above the knee (the usual procedure) is almost always avoided.

Since we know that, in a diabetic, even the tissues in the terminal degrees of arteriosclerosis can be salvaged, it is logical to assume that the tissues affected to a lesser degree, perhaps not yet severe enough to cause symptoms, can also be reclaimed by vitamin E therapy, preferably reinforced with megavitamin C.

One patient who had been a diabetic for many years and had marked hardening of the arteries in the retinas of both eyes with old and recent hemorrhages, had such deterioration of sight that he had been forced to retire from work. On 1,600 IU of vitamin E a day, his eyesight gradually improved. He was able to return to his old job and carried on perfectly well with his correspondence and all other office work.

On one particular occasion this man had broken his glasses so he had made a date with his eye doctor as well as doctors at a Toronto clinic he frequently went to. At the clinic, for some reason, on that day they asked him all about his symptoms. When he said his eyesight had improved noticeably, they examined his eyes. The doctor looked into his eye grounds with the ophthalmoscope. The doctor then took off his glasses and wiped them, wiped the lens of the ophthalmoscope and looked at the man's retinas again. He called in his colleagues and they looked at the patient's eyes and asked him what he had been doing. He told them he had been taking vitamin E.

The patient left there and went to his eye doctor to get his glasses replaced. The eye doctor, of course, did an ophthalmoscopic examination and he did what the clinic doctor had done. He wiped his glasses and the lens of the ophthalmoscope and called in his partner for verification. He said he'd never seen anything like it before; it was just a beautiful disappearance of most of the signs of diabetic retinas. He confirmed the resolution of the hemorrhages and the decrease in the arteriosclerotic changes.

One of the main dangers for diabetics is physical traumatic injury that damages the tissues already low in circulation and therefore low in oxygen and this can lead to gangrene and eventually to amputation. We have had a great many diabetics who had gangrene when they first came to us, but in each one all the tissue ever lost was the tissue that was dead on the first day we saw the patient.

I remember a seventy-nine-year-old woman who called me to see her in London, Ontario. She had a totally dead great toe. It was black and it had become infected. This is so-called wet gangrene which is very dangerous because, with the infection and the lack of blood supply, it spreads very rapidly. I saw her at her home at the request of her family physician. I had him supervise the insulin, the diet, and general treatment, but I put her on a large dose of vitamin E, 1,600 IU daily.

The infection and the gangrene had extended into her foot. (An English paper I once read said that gangrene beyond the base of the great toe always progresses to amputation above the knee.) We put her on vitamin E treatment with the result that she lost the affected great toe by self-amputation. Self-amputation merely means that the tissues which are still alive at the junction of the dead cells eat away the dead tissue and eventually a line of separation develops and the appendage, in this case the toe, drops off by itself. In some cases it is necessary to cut back the bone a little because it projects, but healing is prompt and complete.

This lady lost no more than her great toe and she walks perfectly well. She didn't have to go to a hospital and she didn't lose any money to hospitalization or drugs. She is still very much alive at age ninety or so, taking 1,600 IU of vitamin E per day.

At the Shute Institute we have had patients from every state in the Union, including Hawaii and Alaska, every province in Canada and from the Isle of Capri, Switzerland, Ireland, England, Ceylon, Australia, and New Zealand.

One patient was the first governor of Alaska when it achieved statehood, and the head of a university there. He was a diabetic so severely ill the first time he came to us that he had a nurse with him who never left his side during the trip.

He was going blind, he was developing gangrene, as I remember it, he had hypertension and I think he had had one heart attack.

That time he could barely walk. He arrived by plane and took a taxi to the Institute and went home the same way. The next time he came back for a check-up he still had the nurse with him, but he was able to take a side trip to Washington, D.C., en route to us, to conduct state business. The third time he came back he came by himself, after spending a week or so working in Washington. He never needed to come back again. He lost his symptoms and lowered his insulin requirement and lived comfortably for far longer than his expectation when he first came to the Shute Institute.

When I think of the slow acceptance of vitamin E, I like to remember that it took more than eight years for insulin to be accepted by establishment medicine. Eight years after it had been first used successfully on a human patient it was still not being used in the great Cleveland Clinic. A doctor friend of mine reported that the Cleveland Clinic's authority on diabetes insisted that insulin hadn't been proven effective, and that it hadn't been standardized. He considered life-saving insulin dangerous and refused to use it. Penicillin had similar difficulties in being recognized as a lifesaver.

Now, I don't believe many, if any, doctors ever considered vitamin E dangerous, but plenty were, and are, skeptical of its value as a treatment. However, a great many doctors have become interested in vitamin E therapy and use it the same as it is used at the Shute Institute, and I have every reason to expect that acceptance to increase.

## Multiple Sclerosis

MS has a wide variety of symptoms and it is difficult to diagnose in its early stages. It usually progresses so slowly that
the patient may live up to twenty years after the initial symptom. It is also characterized by spontaneous remissions of
varying lengths.

This is a disease of the nervous system with patchy destruc-
tion of the myelin tissue which sheaths the brain and spinal
cord, and with loss of function in the peripheral nerves of
these areas. Minor changes in eyesight or spells of weakness
of muscles, slight stiffness of a limb, dizziness, or difficulties
with bladder control, are the common symptoms at the beginning.

Since areas of different sizes and locations are characteristic,
it is often not until the disease is well advanced that the
diagnosis is finally established. No specific therapy is known
and spontaneous remissions, sometimes lasting for long periods
of time, make evaluation of treatment difficult. In the later
stages of MS the victims become relatively helpless, and eventually bed patients subject to bedsores and urinary tract infections, since by this time they are usually incontinent of bladder
and bowel.

In the early days of the Shute Institute several such patients
came to us. Often, these patients had been to the "great name"
clinics and specialists, with no encouraging results. However,
we have never turned anyone away, no matter how hopeless
the situation seemed to be. Some would say the results we
saw after vitamin E therapy were actually instances of spontaneous remission. I don't believe they were. I can only
describe what happened and let others decide for themselves.

A man with multiple sclerosis came to us with his wife in a

van which had been fitted out as living quarters. (This was long before the days of the auto-home.) They had been touring the continent in search of help, but had had no success. On being treated with vitamin E, this man apparently made a worthwhile recovery. He was able to go back to work in his business, which consisted of a poultry farm with a large egg route.

A resident of London, Ontario, suffering from multiple sclerosis, had reached the stage where he was confined to the house. He called me in and I treated him with 600 IU daily of vitamin E. He responded so well that he became a familiar sight to me, working on his lawn and in his flower garden, as I passed his home on my way to and from my office each day.

On a trip to Bermuda to judge the first International Dog Show ever held there, I met the sister of the club treasurer, and she was a multiple sclerosis patient. She still managed to run her household (with the help of a companion) from a wheelchair to which she had been confined for nearly four years. She had a continuous in-dwelling catheter. After treatment with vitamin E, which I prescribed, she was up and walking and able to resume painting, a hobby which her illness had forced her to discontinue.

Dr. John T. Hauch, head of the medical department at St. Joseph's Hospital in Toronto, touched on MS and vitamin E in a paper published in the *Canadian Medical Association Journal* (July 15, 1957) entitled "A New Treatment for Resistant Bed Sores." In it he reported on the results obtained in four cases, one of which involved a patient with advanced multiple sclerosis, whose MS symptoms were of five years' duration. This paper is particularly interesting because the patient was given 1,600 IU of vitamin E daily by mouth, and her pressure sores were treated in three different ways: (1) with vitamin E ointment to the worst, (2) petroleum jelly to the next largest, and (3) any treatment the hospital could devise, to the smallest.

They all healed but the worst one healed first, the second largest next, and the smallest last. Moreover, the doctors became very excited when the patient began to regain the use of paralyzed muscles, and when she began to sit up and take enough notice of her appearance to use lipstick and take an interest in life again.

Once more let it be understood that the cells of the gray matter of the brain and spinal cord cannot be replaced once they are dead. The only way vitamin E can help is to decrease the oxygen need in the cells surrounding the area, that is, in cells which are still not dead but are not functioning well because of a lack of oxygen, whatever the reason. Vitamin E has the special ability to return these areas, which can be quite substantial in size, to normal function.

# Acute and Chronic Nephritis

Acute glomerulonephritis, a common kidney disorder, is one of three conditions in which 400 to 1,600 IU of vitamin E will halt and completely reverse all clinical and laboratory evidence of the disease within two to four days. (Acute thrombophlebitis and acute rheumatic fever are the other two.)

Acute nephritis is like rheumatic fever in that it is almost always triggered by an infection in the tonsils or nasopharynx or in the upper respiratory tract. Then it takes hold either through a toxin, or the bugs themselves, circulating through the bloodstream. If they involve the heart, acute rheumatic fever can develop; if they involve the kidney, acute nephritis is likely.

If vitamin E is given at the onset of the ailment the cure is complete enough so that there is no danger of developing a chronic problem. Less than 5 percent of acute nephritis patients die of that ailment but some of the 95 percent remaining do go on to the chronic phase. Many of these show no clinical evidence of nephritis for twenty or thirty years or more, except for slight albumen and a few red blood cells in the urine. However, in some of these patients, kidney function slowly decreases until such symptoms as excessive urination at night, elevated blood urea nitrogen, anemia, and high blood pressure develop.

The determining factor is the condition of the capillary loops (glomeruli) which are surrounded by a structure that collects the waste products and fluid that become the urine to be excreted. These glomeruli become swollen, with the passages narrowed by overgrowth of the living cells and the presence of pus cells which may completely close the vessels off. These masses of cells, with or without clotting of the blood in some of the capillary loops, may cause these glomeruli to die. With the damage to the capillary walls, fluid leaks out into the tissues between the cells and prevents the passage of oxygen and essential nutrients into the cells. The number of glomeruli destroyed determines the result.

The effect of vitamin E here is threefold:

It restores the capillary permeability to normal and restores the return flow of blood from the glomeruli, allowing this blood to remove the toxic substances.

It removes the fluid between the cells and that reduces the swelling of the kidney. This is very important, since the kidney is surrounded by a strong capsule which prevents its swelling beyond a certain point. If fluid continues to accumulate and increases the swelling beyond this point, the only possible result is a compression of the tissues, especially the glomeruli, which results in their death.

The third effect is that clotting of blood inside the capillaries of the glomeruli is prevented. So the glomerulonephritis is completely reversed and the patient recovers rapidly while avoiding the damage that would otherwise lead to a chronic nephritis.

Victims of chronic nephritis who have developed serious symptoms can sometimes be helped dramatically, depending on the number of glomeruli left. (Remember, these symptoms do not appear until kidney function has dropped below 20 percent.) As long as the glomerulus is alive its function can be largely restored by vitamin E treatment. Improved glomerular function is followed by the disappearance of symptoms. This valuable use for vitamin E was first reported by me in the *Urologic and Cutaneous Review* (60: 679, 1946) and has been confirmed in nineteen papers by others since.

The first patient I treated was a girl of about eight or nine who went to a Canadian summer resort near our town and happened to be in the cottage next to a doctor friend of mine. She had a cold and started to have swelling of her face and extremities. The girl was taken down to the Hospital for Sick Children in Toronto where she was kept for some time. Eventually she recovered to some degree on a diet and the diet only.

The doctors decided that her sinuses were responsible for the nephritis but that she was too sick to withstand surgery on the sinuses at that stage. The child was sent home and was under the care of a very good doctor who looked after her for some months. Her mother met my doctor friend on the street one day and he asked how the little girl was. The mother said the child was doing poorly. My friend suggested that the girl be brought to me.

When she came into my office she had a round swollen face, edema of the extremities all the way up to her hips, and her urine was typical of an acute and subacute nephritis with red cells and white cells and casts. I started her on 400 IU of vitamin E, thinking the damage was already too great and that probably nothing we could do would help her. Fortunately, she recovered completely.

The second case I had was a little boy about five. His father, an optometrist, was just opening an office. He was still fixing the place and had not yet put in a bathroom. One day when the little boy was visiting his dad he had to void, so he used a basin in the sink. His father noticed that the boy's urine was red.

I was the family doctor, so naturally they phoned me and brought the boy to my office at once. I checked him and found he had acute nephritis. I put him on vitamin E and he was a perfectly normal child within forty-eight hours, in every way normal, and he has been normal ever since.

At this stage of the development of vitamin E treatment, our dosage was in the 400-600 IU range. In 1950 Dr. Ochsner had a paper printed in the *Journal of the American Medical Association* describing the results of using 600 IU doses. We decided then that if he could use 600 IU doses we could do so safely. Today I would prescribe 800 to 1,600 IU for this ailment.

# Rheumatoid Arthritis

This type of arthritis ranges from mild to very severe. Deformities may develop, particularly flexion contractures, and, of course, swelling in the affected joints is characteristic. Tenderness is present in nearly all active joints, and similar involvement of the small joints of hands and feet, wrists, elbows, and ankles on both sides is typical.

Various treatments for rheumatoid arthritis have been tried but the number of chronic cases evident in the general population is the best evidence of their ineffectiveness in most cases.

Vitamin E is by no means a cure, but it has much to contribute. The first patient we treated for this disease appeared at the Shute Institute soon after our return from the First International Conference on Vitamin E in Montreal, Canada, where Burgess and Pritchard of the Montreal General Hospital showed how they healed ulcers using an ointment made of vitamin E in petrolatum and applied locally.

Our patient was a professional seamstress and the rheumatoid arthritis involving the fingers of both hands had become so painful that she could no longer sew. My brother spoke to her for a few moments, then on impulse handed her a sample of the new vitamin E ointment we had just received for testing and told her to rub it into her fingers. Since she couldn't work she went to visit her daughter in Niagara Falls. When this woman returned to the institute in about two weeks her hands were completely mobile and useful. She had full use of her fingers and was very pleased and happy and so were we.

We have used vitamin E ointment in many cases since and find that it usually reduces the swelling, takes away the tenderness, and increases mobility of the affected joints. However, some swelling remains and complete healing seldom occurs. It is a very useful agent, used locally. The ointment is rubbed in gently for ten minutes at bedtime, followed by heat for ten minutes.

Incidentally, one of the most successful cases we know of was that of one of England's industrialists, head of one of England's big three automobile companies. He had established a scholarship fund which brought graduate medical doctors from the various countries of the British Empire to England. An acquaintance suggested that this businessman try vitamin E ointment for his arthritis. He was one of the few cures, or near cures, and remarked that he had more help from the friend who told him about vitamin E than from all the doctors he had helped with his scholarships.

**Steroids**  Corticosteroids and their synthetic sisters are widely used in treating a variety of ailments, including rheumatoid arthritis, because of the drugs' antiinflammatory, antiallergic, and lympholytic properties. However, this is a group of drugs that comes with many serious side effects such as fluid retention, peripheral edema and congestive heart failure, and areas of inflammation. Due to these drugs, calcium may be lost from bones, and gastric or duodenal ulcers can occur. The many psychological complications they can lead to include euphoria, depression, agitation, insomnia, delusions, and hallucinations.

The treatment of arthritis or any other ailment with steroids must take these risks into account. That's where vitamin E may prove useful. Two reports suggest that vitamin E may enhance the effect of steroid therapy, allowing for much smaller and therefore safer dosage levels to be used. At the same time, the drug in combination with vitamin E is of increased value.

A report presented to the Japanese Rheumatism Society by Dr. Takefum Morotomi and Dr. Sadao Kira concerned the treatment of rheumatoid arthritis. They stated that the addition of vitamin E allowed the reduction of the steroid dosage to approximately one-third, with a great reduction in side effects. They also reported that the addition of vitamin E improved the circulation in the extremities, and that patients commonly told of losing the "cold feeling" in their limbs.

The other report suggests a similar symbiosis. Drs. P. M. DeSanctis and G. A. Furey reported in the *Journal of Urology* that 85 percent of patients suffering from Peyronie's disease (scarring of one of the three main muscles of the penis with contractures and resulting deformities) were helped by steroids, but that 100 percent were helped when vitamin E was added.

The use of steroids by doctors is widespread, often to treat conditions for which they have no other treatment to suggest, or sometimes to arrest a dangerous condition until other, slower medication has had time to act. In any case, if steroids are necessary, they should be used in the smallest dose that will give the desired results when supplemented with vitamin E.

# Stomach Ulcers and Various Intestinal Troubles

Shortly after the close of World War II, a conference on vitamin E was held in Rochester, New York. At that meeting a paper on the subject of ulcers in the stomach of rats was presented by the biochemists of the Distillation Products Division of the Eastman Kodak Company. They reported that they could produce ulcers in the stomachs of rats in a variety of ways, but no matter how produced, the ulcers would heal promptly when treated with vitamin E.

The rat stomach is quite different structurally from the human stomach, but of course this experiment interested many of the clinicians present, the Shutes in particular. In the course of treating a large number of patients, inevitably we saw some who had a history of duodenal or gastric ulcer. When we first began treating patients with vitamin E (at that time only synthetic E was used), some of them complained of gastric distress—"gas" or a feeling of fullness or pressure—so we carefully warned our ulcer patients to be sure to report any untoward stomach distress.

Dr. George Dowd of Worcester, Massachusetts, was especially interested in this peptic ulcer report. He is the one who first noted improvement in the eyesight of patients using vitamin E at his geriatric clinic. In the six-month interval between the Rochester meeting and the next one held at Columbia University, he put two new ulcer patients—one on the obese side, the other unduly thin—on vitamin E. The heavy one was also on a reducing diet; the other was getting a supplement of complete protein (meaning meat, whole cereal grains, and milk) to help build him up. The fat man was not helped; the ulcer of the patient who was given the supplement healed rapidly.

At the Columbia meeting, a group from Columbia University presented a new paper on the subject of peptic ulcers in rats. This group had tried to reproduce the same results as those obtained by the Rochester group, but, although they were able to induce the ulcers, the ulcers did not heal when treated with vitamin E. However, when the experimenters added casein, the protein of milk, to the rats' diet, the ulcers promptly healed.

That was what Dr. Dowd had found in his two patients. The patient who received casein (in the form of skim milk) with his vitamin E is the one whose ulcer healed.

This has turned out to be a most useful piece of knowledge. Now, whenever a patient has any epigastric discomfort on a large dose of vitamin E, all we need to do is have him take his vitamin E half way through his meals and take three teaspoonfuls of skim milk powder in a little milk or water after each meal. It really works!

An interesting conjecture about the ulcer diet, or Sippy diet, used for many years which required the patient to take milk and cream every hour during his waking hours: could it be that years ago, before we sank to today's critical level of insufficient vitamin E in our foods, we were getting enough E so that the casein in milk of the Sippy diet combined with the vitamin E to produce the results claimed for the Sippy diet?

For thirty years my practice has been limited to cardio-vascular-renal diseases, so my experience with the treatment of peptic ulcer is understandably limited. However, I have treated one patient who had one of the three complications of ulcer (perforation, severe stenosis, and recurrent severe hemorrhages) that demand a surgical answer.

When he was told that his ulcer was hemorrhaging once more, and that he needed immediate surgery, he asked for a consultation with me. I urged surgery, but told him about the vitamin E and skim milk powder trick. He insisted on trying that treatment. After warning of the dangers involved in postponing surgery, I cooperated. The patient stopped bleeding within twenty-four hours, and has had no hemorrhages since.

Of course, I realize that one case proves nothing. Still, it was an interesting case and suggests that E plus the protein of milk may well be the best of all nonsurgical treatments for peptic ulcer, since no other treatment of this condition has ever been especially satisfactory.

A very serious disease called Crohn's disease, or ulcerative colitis, occurs in many young men and women. It is usually progressive and the only effective treatment up to now has been the removal of the affected segment of bowel, with the upper portion of the remainder brought out through the abdominal wall. The sad part is that such openings are subject to ulceration and infection of the surrounding tissue. Sadder still is the usual history—a recurrence, often within five years. Fortunately these complications can be controlled with vitamin E applied locally or taken orally in 1,600 IU doses. Now comes a startling report on the apparent heading of the ulcerated bowel left in the body and the removal of all the distressing symptoms and complications in one of the most severe of such cases.

In a letter published in the *Summary* (1974), A. J. DiLiz, of Garden City, Long Island, New York describes the case of a woman with daily diarrhea, up to ten times, rectal hemorrhages, abdominal cramps of violence and frequency, and four large perianal and perineal openings which had been left open since four abscesses had been surgically incised. The terminal part of the ileum and upper part of the colon had been removed for acute intestinal obstruction five years before she was started on vitamin E therapy, 16,000 IU a day.

By the end of four weeks on vitamin E the diarrhea stopped and the fistulous openings in the perianal and perineal areas were reduced to one-half their previous size. Subsequently, the cramps decreased. She became free of pain and could sleep through the night. Five months after treatment was begun, two of the fistulas had closed, and the other two were almost closed. The ten diarrheal bowel movements a day gave way to one solid movement daily. X rays are now negative, no evidence of acute colitis or ulceration in what remains of the ileum or in the colon or rectum.

This startling success in a heretofore virtually untreatable disease suggests that here might well be another useful application of megavitamin therapy. If so, many hundreds of victims of Crohn's disease could be healed without major surgery and thus avoid the inconvenience of colostomy bags attached to the abdomen.

# Healing Diseased Bones

*It is often the case that patients seek vitamin E treatment as a last resort, after they have tried everything else their doctors can think of. I don't mind, for it gives vitamin E a real chance to prove itself. However, I do regret the pain and incapacity such patients suffer before they turn to this treatment. Bone infections that would respond to nothing else have succumbed to vitamin E, as have abnormal calcium deposits. Patients with excessively brittle bones, prone to frequent fractures, have seen the problem vanish when vitamin E was introduced as a treatment.*

## Bone Infections

Very early in my experience with megavitamin E therapy, I dealt with an unusual case involving a war veteran. He had been an officer in the Canadian army when he was injured while riding in a jeep in Italy. The jeep ran over a land mine, killing the driver and leaving the officer with one leg blown off.

At the hospital, fragments of bone and cloth from the officer's pants and underwear were removed from the wound before a mid-thigh amputation. But, presumably, the doctors didn't get all the foreign matter out, because the stump became grossly infected. A reamputation was done, but following this, infection occurred again. A third amputation was performed, but it was also unsuccessful.

When the officer came to me there was a large draining sinus from the bone to the surface of the stump in the very middle of the incision. He could only wear his prosthetic leg for a short interval during the day and the discharge was sufficient to wet through all dressings. The army surgeons had told him that the only solution was yet another amputation. However, his stump was now so short that with another operation it would be too short to accommodate a practical artificial leg. He would have to use a bucket type, in which his stump would have no usefulness in swinging the leg. The soldier's father, a patient of mine, suggested his son come to see me, in the hope that I could do something to help him.

I started the amputee on oral vitamin E and his infection cleared up entirely. All drainage ceased and the stump healed over. Thereafter he was able to wear his prosthesis successfully.

Though I have had a very limited experience with such cases (infection of the bone with draining sinuses opening on the surface) since that one, I have been very pleased with the almost universal improvement in the few cases I did treat. Two of these patients were nurses working at the Ontario Hospital in London. Both had had mastoidectomies performed several years before and had constant drainage since, aggravated with every upper respiratory tract infection.

One of these women attended a lecture I gave on vitamin E at the Shute Institute, and asked if vitamin E would have any effect in her case. Remembering my experience with the army officer, I suggested that it might be worth trying. Her infection cleared completely with vitamin E treatment and even severe head colds did not cause a recurrence.

The other nurse worked in the same large hospital but, curiously enough, the two women had not met, even though they had the same family name. She telephoned me about her draining mastoid sinus, after having heard of the first nurse's success. Unfortunately, this nurse's case did not clear up completely in response to vitamin E, although the drainage lessened and was not exacerbated with head colds as it had been before.

One important factor in such cases is the size of the sinus opening. It must be large enough for complete evacuation of the discharge, and must allow progressive healing from the bone outward. Obviously, this factor was favorable in the first case but not in the second.

Another of my patients had been run over by a coal wagon at the age of nine. One leg was so badly smashed that amputation was advised. His father refused to allow amputation and the boy was two years in the hospital before he could walk again, using the leg fairly well. In the years that followed, several operations had been required to remove bone fragments and for skin grafts.

When this man came to me he had four ulcers in the badly scarred and discolored anterior surface of the leg. These ulcers varied in size and the degree of infection and discharge. Using vitamin E orally and in an ointment locally applied, all four healed completely. During the process, several bone chips were also extruded spontaneously.

## Balancing Calcium Metabolism

Vitamin E therapy is useful, we believe, in speeding up the union of fractures. This is difficult to prove, since there is always a chance that these fractures were about to heal anyway. The inference is that vitamin E favorably influences abnormal calcium metabolism, whether too much calcium is being deposited in tissues or too little.

The following item appeared in a 1947 United Press release. It was especially interesting to me because I had known the surgeon supervising this case (Dr. Compere) when I was the resident in pathology at the University of Chicago Clinics.

Johnny Crowe, ten, whose legs were turning to stone until doctors began a series of medical experiments on them, took his first faltering steps in five years, Friday.

It was the first time on record that such a case had responded to medical treatment. Doctors believed the boy's improvement was due to highly concentrated doses of vitamin E.

Johnny was stricken with the rare disease five years ago. His muscles were turning to stone.

American Medical Association spokesmen said that the disease runs its course until the patient is completely "petrified." There had been cases of recovery where only one muscle was affected. But all of Johnny's muscles were becoming hard.

He was admitted to Children's Memorial Hospital in 1943, able to sit and to crawl, but he could not walk.

Doctors began a series of operations to lengthen the tendons in his legs and to remove deposits of calcium. X-ray therapy was tried but nothing seemed to help until they began experimenting with vitamin E, never used before on this strange disease.

Slowly, Johnny began to recover. His muscles softened, became flexible again.

Friday, with the aid of helping hands, he could walk again for a few steps.

Doctors said they were confident that within two years he would be playing football with the neighborhood boys.

More recent evidence of the ability of vitamin E to remove abnormal calcium deposits is the report of Dr. A. M. Boyd, Chief of Surgery at the University of Manchester, in England. He noted that during his successful use of vitamin E in treating over 1,500 cases of intermittent claudication, x-ray studies showed that abnormal calcium deposits were being removed from the walls of the old sclerotic (hardened) arteries. Conversely, in two cases of *fragilitas osseum* (weak bone) that I treated, where the deposition of calcium was deficient, vitamin E corrected the abnormality when given along with enough calcium and vitamin D to allow for, and this word is important, *normal* calcium deposition.

What happens in the patient with *fragilitas ossium* is that the bones fracture easily, but they heal completely and fairly rapidly. And where they heal, sufficient bone is laid down that they never will break in that spot again.

One of my patients once asked me what could be done about *fragilitas ossium,* because she had a friend whose little daughter suffered from this condition. When the child was born doctors noticed that she wasn't using one leg and they x-rayed it. They found that during delivery the child's leg had been broken. A few months later an older sister was helping the baby to get into those little vests that babies used to wear, and in bringing the arm back to put through the armhole she broke the arm. Another time, the baby was being diapered on a high table and she fell and broke an arm again. And this child was still an infant! I suggested that this baby be given extra vitamin D and calcium and a good daily dose of vitamin E. Some two years later I was speaking at a public meeting in

Detroit and the mother was present with the baby. I met them after the meeting. The mother told me that the child had had no fractures since she began using the supplements. This in spite of several accidents of the type which would have led to a broken bone in a child with this condition.

Another patient I treated, a teenage girl, was going to the university in London, Ontario, and had developed a mild degree of *fragilitas ossium*. I found out about her problem in an odd way. Her father was a heart patient of mine and I was called one night by the wife because this man was having pain in his chest. She wanted me to come and see him because she feared that he might have had another heart attack. I went at once and found that the man had a high fever; it was 102°. or 103°F. I wanted to look at his throat because I was sure tonsillitis or something like it was causing the fever, so I reached into my bag for a tongue depressor and discovered that I had run out of them.

I turned to his wife and asked her to get me a spoon so I could use it to look at his throat. She said, "Wouldn't you rather use a tongue depressor?" With that, she reached into a drawer (we were in his daughter's bedroom where he had flopped on the bed when the pain first hit him) and handed me a tongue depressor. I saw splints and bandages and all manner of equipment in this drawer.

Later I remarked that they appeared to be running a hospital in their home. By way of explanation the wife told me that their daughter had *fragilitas ossium* and they'd become tired of taking her to the surgeon so the girl began to splint her own fractures. For example, she told me, "The other day my daughter was going out the door on her way to school and she turned to say goodbye to me. In doing so she put her hand against the doorjamb and broke her finger, so she just splinted it with a tongue depressor and went off to school."

"She wants to be a minister of the gospel," the mother went on, "and she was out circuit riding in western Canada last year. She went to get on her horse, put her foot into the stirrup, hoisted herself up, and broke her leg."

Nearly all my cardiac patients, and many of my other patients, have a degree of low thyroid activity and this girl was a big, heavy-set redheaded girl. I checked her thyroid. She had had rheumatic fever and she was a marked hypothyroid. I put her on thyroid medication and vitamin E and she has had no fracture since.

This patient did her best to test the treatment when she rode a friend's bike that had English brakes, which were unfamiliar to her. The girl turned a corner, hit a fresh gravel road near the university, applied the brakes, and flew over the handlebars. She was badly scraped and had all sorts of gravel burns, but no fractures.

# Eyesight Improvement

*The positive effect vitamin E often has on eyesight is surely the result of its basic ability to improve circulation everywhere in the body. For that reason we see apparently spontaneous improvement among patients taking vitamin E, in conditions of the eye caused by diabetes, hardening of the arteries, high blood pressure, and general aging. Practitioners treating for some other ailment are amazed when routine examination of the eyes shows a remarkable change for the better.*

## Accidental Discoveries

Following the reports in 1945 on our initial good results with vitamin E, news of our successes was widely published in Canadian and American newspapers. At the instigation of Dr. Paul Dudley White, Dr. George Dowd of Worcester, Massachusetts, flew up to London, Ontario, to investigate our treatment and its results. Dr. Dowd had a twice-weekly geriatric clinic in Boston. On his return from London, he placed all clinic patients on vitamin E. One of the first changes he noticed was an improvement in the eyesight of some of these patients.

On his second visit to us Dr. Dowd was shown several heart patients who had been successfully treated by me. He seemed particularly interested in those who were wearing glasses. When questioned, two of these reported improvement in their eyesight after taking vitamin E for their hearts. When I reported this to my wife who had always been shortsighted, she pointed out that her eyesight had also improved since she began taking vitamin E to maintain her pregnancy. A checkup with her ophthalmologist confirmed an astonishing degree of improvement.

The medical literature has carried more than twenty articles since then, confirming the value of vitamin E as a treatment for ocular diseases. Occasionally one of our patients reports marked improvement in his eyesight. Ophthalmologists to whom we refer patients, or who have been treating our patients, have reported significant improvement in various lesions.

At the International Symposium on Vitamin E held in Minneapolis in 1973, a very important paper was read showing that, on the basis of twenty months' experience with acute stage retrolental fibroplasia, vitamin E caused a decrease in overall incidence and a decrease in both the severity and duration of the acute stage. "Healing appears also to be favorably influenced."

In addition, vitamin E used with vitamin A gave relief to specific eye conditions in cases in which neither alone helped. The same is true with a combination of vitamins E and C.

At the meeting of the International Academy of Preventive Medicine in 1974, Dr. Morgan Raiford of the Atlanta (Georgia) Eye Hospital showed the symposium audience colored slides of the retina in patients with arteriosclerotic changes, whether due to aging, high blood pressure, or diabetes mellitus. He then demonstrated, by a series of such photographs, that vitamin E used with vitamin C actually reversed the arteriosclerotic changes in these cases.

In my own practice I have seen very marked improvement in the eyesight of diabetics who were no longer able to read. Their eyesight returned to almost normal. I hasten to add that although I have seen eyesight degeneration halted, I have also seen eyesight deteriorate in spite of vitamin E treatment.

# Skin-Related Problems

*Topical application of nutrients is a source of some controversy in medical circles. It is safe to say the consensus is that if vitamins do any good at all, it's from the inside, through the system. That may be true as a general rule, but vitamin E penetrates the skin speedily. When it comes to skin trouble, vitamin E applied directly to the site does wonders. It helps to avoid scarring from acne and it goes right to the source of pain to relieve the victims of shingles. The phenomenal results achieved in treating burns—ranging from sunburn to scalding—with applied vitamin E, make it a "must" for every household medicine cabinet.*

# A Home Remedy

Because vitamin E has the ability to decrease the need of oxygen to all cells, to prevent unwanted clotting in blood vessels of all sizes, to open up collateral channels of blood supply, and to directly benefit all collagen fibers, its beneficial effect on such skin lesions as psoriasis and varicose eczema is not surprising.

Vitamin E cream or ointment will actually fill in acne or chicken pox scars on the face, often to the point where they are barely discernible. I know this as a father as well as in the role of clinician. While she was an undergraduate nurse, my daughter Karen had a very severe attack of chicken pox which left several scars on her face and forehead. Vitamin E ointment was rubbed in regularly and the scars disappeared entirely.

My wife Dorothy suffered many cuts around the face from the shattered glass of the windshield in a car accident. Her face was so badly cut up and sore that she couldn't bear to wash it. Instead she applied vitamin E ointment liberally, and within a week her face was healed. There are no scars. Incidentally, I believe that vitamin E is a must for the after-care of all plastic surgery scars.

I know that stretch marks on the abdomen that often follow pregnancy can be prevented or made much less obvious with vitamin E. After two full-term pregnancies with large babies, my daughter Barbara had no stretch marks whatsoever, due, I believe, to her regular intake of vitamin E.

Examples of the practical uses of vitamin E ointment, and of the oil squeezed out of capsules, keep increasing in the medical literature, as well as in lay publications. The direct application of vitamin E from the capsule is credited with clearing up such problems as plantar warts and itching scalp. Several mothers have reported that vitamin E ointment is their favorite remedy for diaper rash. One woman found that the ointment gave relief from a very uncomfortable chronic irritation caused by sweat and clothing under her large and pendulous breasts.

The effect of vitamin E ointment on the common moles which may be present at birth or develop later, can be quite remarkable, but persistence in applying it at night is necessary. Sometimes moles simply drop off, leaving a smooth surface level with the skin.

**Journals Describe Response of More Serious Lesions** The journals devoted to dermatology tell of a variety of skin lesions which respond to vitamin E therapy. Many of the contributions come from Ayers and Mihan of California, who explain how they became interested in vitamin E as a therapeutic agent:

> . . . Milton Stout presented before the Los Angeles Dermatological Society in 1950, a woman with *pseudoxanthoma elasticum,* whose cutaneous and visual impairment were restored to near-normal following administration of vitamin E for a period of one year.
>
> This astounding therapeutic accomplishment in a hitherto untreatable disease led us to carry out a continuing clinical investigation among our private office patients with some highly gratifying results.

He lists the following as responding to vitamin E: *epidermolysis bullosa,* Raynaud's phenomenon with gangrene, *scleroderma, calcinosis cutis,* Darier's disease (in combination with vitamin A), severe types of cutaneous vasculitis, subcorneal pustular dermatosis, benign chronic pemphigus, and some cases of chronic ulcers, *discoid lupus erythematosus* and *granuloma annulare.*

They also noted that vitamin E gave prompt relief to nocturnal leg cramps and various types of muscle cramps, exer-

cise cramps, restless legs syndrome and intermittent claudication, and also one spectacular case of polymyositis, after the
total failure of three immunosuppressive drugs.

**Vitamin E Inserts**    The Canadian manufacturer of one of the
best-known brands of vitamin E was asked if it really was
good for "piles." He telephoned us long distance to ask
about vitamin E for hemorrhoids and about making a vitamin
E suppository. My reply was that it could be useful because
hemorrhoids were really varicose veins, and since vitamin E
often does help varicose veins the suppository just might be a
useful product.

Evan doubted that vitamin E would be useful as a rectal
suppository, but said he would like to see a vaginal suppository
to use as a convenient way of treating atrophic vaginitis and
other such conditions. He had been using vitamin E ointment
to treat such problems and had found it very effective. Vitamin
E suppositories—known as "Vitamin E Inserts"—have been on
the market for years now and are really useful in both areas.

# Leukoplakia

Leukoplakia lesions in mucous membranes demand serious consideration because they are presumed to be precancerous in a fair proportion of cases. When such a lesion occurs in the mucous membrane of the vagina or the mouth, for example, the accepted treatment is to remove any known irritant—if there is one. This does not actually improve the lesion, but the hope is that its progression is slowed. The only other solution known is surgical removal.

My brothers, Evan and Wallace, highly trained obstetricians and gynecologists, have successfully used vitamin E therapy orally and locally in such cases for more than forty years. They reported their early findings in the *Journal of the American Medical Association* (110: 889, 1938). By now their experience is considerable. Though my opportunities to see and treat this condition are limited because of my specialization, I had success in the two cases I did treat.

The first was a forty-seven-year-old man who developed hoarseness due to a nodule which was removed from one vocal cord in June, 1947. At that time both cords showed leukoplakia. The leukoplakia continued to advance and the man developed hoarseness again by November of the same year. That is when he came to see me and vitamin E therapy was begun.

Because the only treatment the doctors had to suggest was a checkup every month, and because I wanted a second opinion about the progress of the lesion, I insisted that he not tell anyone he was on vitamin E. (I have often used this strategem. That way, the patient has my opinion, his own opinion, and that of the specialist he is seeing, of vitamin E's effect.) Three weeks after beginning vitamin E treatment, this man's otorhinolaryngologist told him he had never before seen such improvement, and a month later he said the same thing. The doctor told the patient another checkup wasn't necessary for six months. By June 1949, the vocal cords were pronounced free of all lesions.

The second case was my nurse, with me for over twenty years. She developed leukoplakia of the mucous membranes of upper and lower lips, and the inside of the mouth. This slowly disappeared on megavitamin E, recurred slightly when she reduced her dosage level, and disappeared again when she raised her vitamin E dosage again.

Over one million patients in North America, and about 110,000 new ones each year, have an interruption in the tubes which at their anatomical ends eliminate body wastes. In the most common operation the open end of the proximal bowel is brought out through an incision in the abdominal wall, and a bag is used to catch the body wastes. Unfortunately, the wound in the abdomen is prone to develop infection; it may be very slow to heal, and can become, therefore, a very serious problem.

An article on this subject written by a nurse for *Prevention* magazine (August 1975) describes the success in healing enterostomy wounds with vitamin E applied locally, along with 1,200 to 1,600 IU per day by mouth. The success obtained with vitamin E in this specialized usage at the Pottsville Hospital and Warne Clinic in Pottsville, Pa., encouraged the surgeons there to use vitamin E treatment for hard-to-heal wounds, diabetic ulcers, even cases with gangrene, and decubitis ulcers (bed sores).

# Shingles

*Herpes zoster,* commonly known as "shingles," is a very painful condition. It is essentially a viral infection of sensory
nerves. Typically, there is a linear series of lesions along a
nerve pathway with a series of blisters. Even after the blisters
are gone pain may remain for months or years.

In the acute stage, we have had excellent results with vitamin E ointment rubbed in gently over the nerve root for ten
minutes followed by heat for ten minutes several times a day.
We use tincture *benzoini compositi,* commonly called Friar's
Balsam, to dry up the blisters. We have seen excellent and
rapid results with manipulation by an osteopath. Now along
comes a report by two dermatologists, Ayres and Mihan, in
the *Archives of Dermatology* (108: 885, 1973) reporting on
the treatment with vitamin E of the neuralgia that follows
shingles:

> Two of thirteen patients who had suffered for thirteen
> years and nineteen years respectively, obtained complete,
> or nearly complete, relief from pain using vitamin E.
> Seven more responded similarly, two others were moder-
> ately improved and another two slightly improved. One
> of the patients in the experimental group had angina.
> She was controlled by 1,200 IU per day. She also lost
> her leg cramps.

Another type of *herpes* is the common "cold sore" of the
lips, *herpes labialis.* I have a letter from Dr. Willard T. Greene,
of Norfolk, Virginia. Re *herpes,* he says:

> In my dental work when a patient is worked on for a
> long period of time, I usually follow the treatment with

vitamin E oil applied to lips and mucosa. This prevents
the development of *herpes simplex,* type 1. *Herpes simplex,* the common cold sore, responds very rapidly to the
local application of vitamin C. Better yet is the effect of
powdered ascorbic acid mixed with vitamin E ointment.
Both together work better and faster than either one
alone.

# Burns

The intense pain, the shock, the risk of infection, and the risk of toxemia caused by serious burns, could be avoided in most cases by prompt use of oral vitamin E and vitamin E ointment. Prolonged hospitalization can be avoided, as can much of the skin grafting, always a painful and slow process. The skin contractions that tend to occur after the healing of burns around armpits, neck, groin, and joints are prevented, because scar tissue formed under the influence of vitamin E does not contract and is not tender.

I remember one serious burn case that occurred when a middle-aged woman was opening the family's summer cottage for the season. The spring weather had turned very cold indeed over that weekend, so she went to bed under a pile of blankets but she was still freezing. Her husband boiled water on the wood stove, filled a plastic bottle with it, and put the bottle under the covers as a warmer. The top came off the bottle and the scalding hot water just inundated her left arm and her breasts and abdomen and even her thigh causing third-degree burns at every point of contact.

The woman was in excruciating pain. Her husband and the neighbors actually had to get out of that remote area with a horse-drawn sled. She was rushed to a hospital in Toronto and there she received the usual treatment for burns. The doctors talked about doing early skin grafting on the woman as soon as the wounds started to clear up.

At church on the Sunday following the accident, her husband told me about it. I said, "Well, there is only one treatment for your wife, of course, and that's vitamin E ointment applied to the burned areas and vitamin E by mouth."

The family signed this woman out of the hospital and

brought her to my office the very next day. My nurses spent three and a half hours getting the dressings off. They were adhering to the skin, and the patient just screamed in pain. The nurses covered her lesions with vitamin E ointment and started her on a daily oral intake of 1,600 units of vitamin E by mouth.

In such a case you use pails of vitamin E ointment (actually petroleum jelly as the base for synthetic vitamin E) and mounds of dressings. This patient used to buy vitamin E ointment by the pound. Over this period (about six weeks) she used four or five pounds of vitamin E. She would apply it with a tongue depressor once a day, usually before bedtime, and then put a dressing over it to keep the burns covered continuously.

Those wounds healed completely and without contraction or tenderness. But the remarkable part about it, as far as the husband was concerned, was that instead of having a wife in utter pain, he had a wife who became comfortable immediately when the vitamin E ointment was applied to her burned surfaces and remained so throughout the rest of the recovery period. She showed excellent results, never needed grafting, and full function returned in every way.

Domestic burns, sunburn, chemical burns, x-ray and radium burns—all types respond to vitamin E therapy. The results are almost always astounding to those seeing them for the first time. Certainly every home and all industrial plants where burns can occur, should have E ointment available.

The contrast between the simple, effective treatment of severe sunburn with vitamin E ointment and the routine treatment for this condition is best illustrated by a question and answer on the subject which appears in *Medical Tribune* (July 23, 1973). The consultant was Dr. Irwin I. Lubowe, clinical professor of dermatology, New York Medical College; attending dermatologist, Metropolitan Hospital Center, New York; author, *The Modern Guide of Skin Care* (New York: E. P. Dutton & Co., 1973).

"What are your recommendations for the treatment of sunburn?"

"The treatment of acute painful sunburn requires the services of a physician. He will suggest compresses of boric acid or Burow's solution, the internal use of anti-histamines and corticosteroids, the injection of a depo-corticosteroid, and corticosteroid creams or spray locally. Topical preparations containing ethyl aminobenzoate must be used with caution because of possible cutaneous sensitization, although they give relief due to anesthetiz-ing the nerve ends. Occasionally codeine or meperidine is necessary for the relief of the severe pain."

Two severe cases of sunburn treated with vitamin E will illustrate the contrast. One of our nurses, a very light blonde, fell asleep on the beach on the first good Sunday in spring and was so badly burned that, although she came to work Monday morning, she was obviously very ill. She was running a fever and had a severe headache. We covered the extensive burn areas with vitamin E ointment, put a sheet over her, and left her to rest in the side room of my office. She fell asleep almost immediately, and within two hours she felt perfectly well—no headache, no fever—and returned to work. Al-though the burn was about twenty hours old before the vitamin E ointment was applied, she did not blister.

The other case involved the president of a pharmaceutical company who sustained a severe sunburn after spending most of the day building an outdoor barbecue while dressed only in a pair of shorts. This man seized the occasion to demon-strate the effect of vitamin E ointment on burns for some of his medical clients. He spread the ointment on one side of his body, leaving the other side untreated. By the next day he had many large and medium-size blisters on the untreated side, but there was no evidence of the burn on the side where vitamin E had been applied.

# The Slow Road to Acceptance

*The times we've been tempted to give up on achieving acceptance for vitamin E were fewer than you might expect. The reason, I think, is that in the beginning we Shutes were too naive to foresee the struggle we were in for. At first, we couldn't imagine that anyone would want to resist a treatment we knew so well to be safe and effective. Later, we simply couldn't let this truly remarkable sustance succumb to a hostile bureaucracy. Now, at last, our faith that vitamin E would eventually prove itself is being vindicated. Every day more of our colleagues are prescribing it and urging others to do so too.*

## Our Faith Has Been Justified

It must be very difficult for the average person to understand how something as effective as vitamin E treatment can take so long to be accepted by orthodox medical men as a treatment for all who need it. We Shutes were really naive. We expected that the discovery of an effective treatment for cardiovascular diseases would be welcomed, not only for the rapid and significant improvement it affords but also for its promise in preventing heart disease and associated circulatory diseases in the first place. Moreover, we knew then, and it is evident now, that there was and is no alternative. Treatment has always been focused on diagnosis, the often ineffective palliation of the symptoms, and the complications of existing disease, all with no hope of prevention.

We should have known better, for we were familiar with the history of medicine and knew of the treatment invariably meted out to innovators in the medical field. The fact that our experiences were similar to so many others—we knew the inside story of Banting's difficulties since my brother was a contemporary of the group involved in it all—was poor consolation. The lives of thousands were at stake. We were thinking of the unnecessary cardiac surgery, the needless leg pains and cramps and unnecessary amputations, the persisting varicose ulcers that could have been healed, the burn victims suffering without cause, the thousands of unnecessary skin grafts, the painful contracting scars that could have been avoided, but above all the needless heart attacks.

It is no consolation that this same situation has existed throughout the ages, with every medical advance. Similar stories readily come to mind. For example, the cardiologist, internist, and family physician each use digitalis. How many know that digitalis was not used for its cardiac effect for 100 years after Withering published his monograph on the foxglove? Or that the sulfonamides took twelve years to achieve acceptance?

We have experienced some peculiar contradictions. For example, a famous classmate of mine, a recognized expert in vascular and cardiac surgery, refused to appear on TV or radio to discuss vitamin E. And when he was questioned for a magazine article, he hedged by saying only that ". . . there are enough intelligent people around who feel they have been helped by vitamin E so that, at least, an open-minded, scientific study of its value is warranted." We have a copy of a letter written by this doctor saying that he had been using vitamin E for the treatment of peripheral vascular disease since 1948, still recommends it in what he considers adequate doses to a fair number of his patients, and even recommended it to a patient in another city by mail. He had even urged a patient to come to me for treatment of his heart condition.

The public finds it hard to understand how a physician can know vitamin E works, use it on his patients for twenty-four years, and be afraid to say so! Such is the power of the Establishment. It so often makes dishonest men out of its membership—especially those with university appointments.

The first reaction to our announcement of our discoveries concerning vitamin E came from two cardiologists and a researcher who said, for publication, that vitamin E was useless and could not do what the Shutes claimed it had done. This was before they knew what vitamin E was, before they treated a single patient with it, or before they even saw a single patient who had been treated.

And think of the effect of the many negative statements in magazines, books, and many newspapers, denying the medical use of megavitamin E. Consider Dr. Olson's appearance before a meeting of the American Heart Association with a paper in which he stated that vitamin E had no value in treating heart disease, but was *useful in treating patients with intermittent claudication*. Surely many present must have spotted the blatant contradiction: intermittent claudication is the result of deficient blood supply to muscles due to arteriosclerotic narrowing of vessels to the legs, the exact parallel to a similar state in the heart due to arteriosclerotic narrowing of the coronary arteries. Dr. Olson must have known that Dr. A. M. Boyd, professor of surgery at the University of Manchester, had published proof in 1963 (*J. Angiology* 14: 198, 1963) and that Knut Haeger had confirmed this in a paper published in Vascular Diseases 5: 199, 1968—that vitamin E does, in fact, prevent heart attacks and death from heart failure.

Naturally, the cardiologists who opposed E treatment and refused to use it find it hard to back down now.

The unthinking and unreasoning attitude of the majority of the doctors turned out by our medical schools, their inability to think for themselves, to believe their own eyes and ears or to accept anything that wasn't taught them in medical schools, is strikingly evident in the experience of Dr. John T. Hauch, (M.D., B.Sc., Ph.D.). He carried out spectacular work on bed sores, and published his findings in the *Canadian Medical Association Journal* (77: 125-28, July 15, 1957). The cases were so remarkable that the superintendent of the hospital began to "suggest" to doctors who had such cases, that they transfer them to Dr. Hauch's service. His efforts to interest the doctors in vitamin E treatment were conspicuously unsuccessful as witness the following letter written November 18, 1964, seven years later. Dr. Hauch was the physician-in-chief of the Department of Medicine.

> I am writing you regarding the present situation at St. Joseph's Hospital re vitamin E which you have so generously donated over the past few years, for carrying on with the treatment of ulcers.
>
> The unfortunate part is that the surgeons have not supported this project as well as I would have liked to see, in fact they have been very reticent in transferring cases to me.
>
> This situation is somewhat unfortunate because the reluctance here permeated to the balance of the medical

staff as well. Despite the fact that on several occasions I have reviewed our work to the group as a whole, showing the advantages of this type of therapy, and even on one occasion had Mr. M—— join me in this endeavour, but with no outstanding response.

It is interesting to note that the value of vitamin E in this type of condition is apparently shared by the Interne Staff, since many have gone out and continued to use it in treating similar cases in their practice.

Regardless of the above factors I still feel there is a definite place for vitamin E in medical therapeutics and shall continue to use it and continue to advocate its value in cases of decubitus and arteriosclerotic ulcers.

In spite of all this, we have faith in the medical profession. Evan and I have spurned numerous chances to gain substantial financial benefits by commercial involvement with the manufacture or sale of vitamin E. Instead, we have proceeded in every ethical way to tell the profession about our findings in the use of megavitamin E to treat human disease. We realized early that this was the most important medical discovery of the twentieth century, since it is a powerful treatment and prophylaxis for this century's number one killer, and its associated diseases.

Our faith has been justified. Fortunately, there are many perceptive and courageous doctors who have accepted the scientific evidence available, and have not only used vitamin E as a treatment themselves, but have advocated its use among their confreres.

# Our Duty Is Done

*The challenge was difficult, but the spiritual rewards were great. It fell to us to present to the world a new tool for healing. Vitamin E needed to be proven to the satisfaction of practicing physicians. We saw that as our responsibility. Now we can pass the torch to others, for we have accomplished that task. Modern medicine can no longer ignore the performance of vitamin E and its potential for still wider uses.*

# The Fundamental Courage to Fight It Out

It is unlikely that I will write another book on vitamin E. The need for authoritative information will not cease, but there are now enough people interested in vitamin E treatment to carry on what we Shutes started so long ago. So we can leave that duty to them. This fills our hearts and souls and minds with deep satisfaction.

It would have been so easy to have bowed out and to have abandoned vitamin E when we elicited unexpected, violent, and unreasoning opposition, or to have given our research over to the ambitious university bureaucrats who attempted to steal it from us. They may well have gone further and faster in the beginning, but it really needed men with fundamental integrity and genuine interest in their patients to carry on the work.

The thousands who flocked to us from literally all over the civilized world, from every state in the Union, every Province in Canada, from the British Isles and the shrinking British Empire, from Ceylon, the Isle of Capri, Switzerland, and the islands—and have received help where there was no help—these are our satisfactions. These also have made it impossible for the philistines to ignore vitamin E and the final capitulation appears to be near at hand. Indeed, many of the enemies of vitamin E have already surrendered, as shown in these pages.

I am so glad our heritage gave us the fundamental courage to fight it out. We may be the first to beat the Establishment. Witness the letters on vitamin E therapy accepted for publication in the *Journal of the American Medical Association* and the scientific exhibit at the American Medical Association Convention at Atlantic City in June, 1975. We have experienced the jealousies and hatreds of little men, the conspiracies of members of the profession controlling the medical journals and the annual scientific conventions; have even had our families threatened by anonymous phone calls. We have had attempts to keep us from membership on hospital staffs.

However, we have also had experiences granted to very few physicians in the entire history of medicine, namely, involvement in a medical discovery of great importance. We have been able to do, for the first time, what no other physician has ever been able to do. We have returned eyesight to patients where there has been only the prospect of blindness, have restored circulation and life to limbs which no one else could save, have healed ulcers which no one else could heal, have restored chronic invalids to normal, active, productive lives and prolonged these lives for years and years beyond anyone's expectation.

We have healed burns without the necessity for prolonged, exceedingly painful, grafting of skin. We have taken a pitiful, emaciated, dying boy after ten unsuccessful attempts to graft skin on his extensive wounds and returned him to normal activity. In this case we were able to do what no one else has ever done—return legs with extreme degrees of flexion contractures of many months duration, to normal function. This is but a small fraction of what we have been able to do.

Latterly, we have seen the concepts we first enunciated, of the various actions of megavitamin E, applied by other bold imaginative clinicians, to many and various other disease entities in their specialties. Many of these have been described in this book.

We may well have been the pioneers in megavitamin therapies. The uses of megavitamins are being explored in more and more medical centers.

We have walked with giants in the scientific world, and with them have influenced many physicians to embrace a whole new type of practice—adding to crisis medicine the methods of disease prevention. These men recognize that nutrition has not been taught thoroughly in any medical school on this continent. They are aware that, unfortunately, the vast majority of physicians, through no fault of their own, know little more about diet and nutrition than the average high school student, in some cases, not as much.

These doctors of the new breed prevent disease, or are able to diagnose conditions in their early stages when they can be reversed and then prevented. They don't wait until the conditions threaten life and are irreversible. Many of these doctors are young, are not impressed by the establishment, and are breaking new ground in medicine. They have welcomed the help of megavitamin therapy and of supplemental amino acids and trace minerals. They have learned to use them correctly, and therefore, successfully. Of course, all other useful forms of treatment are available to them as well, and are used when indicated.

Originally, we believed that the hope for megavitamin E therapy lay in submitting our results to our profession for objective evaluation. Therefore we proceeded through regular medical channels in every way we knew. It was agonizingly slow. We did not, at this time, realize the power of the public. Fortunately, the publication of a book about vitamin E by a layman, and the frequent references to our work in one or two health magazines, interested large numbers of the public who were then anxious for more authentic information. That is the reason for the books I've written. The response has been far greater than ever expected and they have certainly done more for the acceptance of vitamin E therapy in the last five years than all our well-intentioned publications for the medical profession in twenty-five!

As a result, it was reliably estimated three or four years ago, that between thirty and thirty-five million Americans were taking vitamin E in megadoses. One result was that approximately 10,000 middle-aged American males were saved from death by cardiac disease in one year. I am certain that vitamin E and vitamin E only is responsible for the sudden decrease in deaths from heart disease. It will continue as more and more people become acquainted with the preventive aspect of vitamin E therapy.

That is just one of the areas where vitamin E therapy has made a major impact in the health and lives of people. It has already become obvious that with the ever-spreading use of vitamin E, here at last lies hope for a better world.

# Letters

*Over the years we have received thousands of letters from patients and doctors commenting on the usefulness of vitamin E in treating a wide variety of ailments. These are spontaneous evidence of the happy results achieved.*

# Skin Disorders

Here are a few excerpts from the many thousands of letters I have received about the effects of vitamin E. Obviously, these people have written to me in confidence so I have deleted names and addresses.

### Skin Problems

Your name has been given to me in connection with an article that appeared in the *Canadian Medical Association Journal* dated June 6, 1964 with reference to *epidermolysis bullosa* [a skin disease characterized by a severe and chronic outbreak of blisters and boils].

I have just finished reading an article that appeared in the February, 1971 issue of *Nature's Way* that tells of Dr. Wilson's successful treatment of this rare disease using vitamin E.

My six-month-old son (first child) was born with *epidermolysis bullosa*. He has recently been discharged from the N.Y.U. Medical Center in New York City where he was a patient for nearly three months. During that time he was treated with cortisone and prednisone which proved to be ineffective and much too dangerous.

Our doctor's recommendation was that the baby be placed in a children's hospital for chronic diseases. After a great deal of deliberation my husband and I decided against this and since then have been attempting to give him the love and extensive nursing care that he needs at home.

Upon his discharge from N.Y.U., Dr. Chester A. Swinyard, professor of rehabilitation medicine at the Institute of Rehabilitation Medicine, became very interested in our case and recommended the use of zinc sulfate of which my son is presently taking 100 mg. daily. This has proved to be somewhat effective in the healing process of the skin. He is also taking the usual multi-vitamins and an iron supplement (3 ccs. daily).

The report of Dr. Wilson's success with vitamin E has given me new hope.

Dr. Shute, I would sincerely appreciate your advising me as to how this treatment can be made available to my son and to what the necessary dosage is for a child of this age. . . .

I sent a reprint of the original Wilson article (H. D. Wilson, *Canadian Medical Association Journal,* 901-1315, 1964) on April 27, and on September 30, the mother wrote as follows:

———————————•———————————

. . . Eric is now one year old and is presently taking 2,000 IU [of alpha tocopherol] daily. I have seen a tremendous improvement in his skin condition and he is developing into a beautiful, bright, and extremely happy child. My dermatologist agrees with me.

. . . I would like to thank you kindly for all your help. Some day perhaps Eric and I will be in Canada and we will come to see you and thank you in person.

———————————•———————————

I was born with a *hemangioma* (birthmark) on my face. It covers my left eye, forehead, cheek, nose, and upper part of my left lip.

As my sister, who is a medical doctor, read your book on vitamin E, she thought it would be advisable that I take vitamin E. I started with 400 units a day for a period of six months, then increased to 600, and since August to date I am taking 800 units per day. . . .

During the first six months I was taking vitamin E I did not notice any change on my *hemangioma,* but suddenly I started noting that it was fading out little by little and right now it has faded out almost one centimeter all around this birthmark. At the same time that I was taking vitamin E, orally, my sister ordered vitamin E

ointment from Canada and I applied it on my face. . . .
I think the birthmark started disappearing since I started
applying the ointment and taking the vitamin E. . . .

─────────────────•●•─────────────────

Years ago, by chance, I bought your first medical book
on cardiovascular disorders and sent it to my father, a
retired surgeon and medical missionary to China. That
book kept him alive for six or seven years, although he
had a very bad heart. Since then I have been preaching
about vitamin E.

On the evening of May 4, 10:15 P.M., while Bob
was getting ready to turn a valve of fluorine gas under
400 pounds pressure, it exploded in his hand (fortunately
he was on a stepladder), blowing him to the floor in
flames. He was taken to the hospital. Three plastic
surgeons, his family doctor, and the hospital doctor were
called, but none of them knew how to treat fluorine burns.
The wrong neutralizer was almost used; however, Bob
was alert enough to hear and tell them not to use it. They
had to go to Air Products Company and pick up the cor-
rect neutralizer to stop the burning. It was 12:35 A.M.
that the neutralizer was put on his arm.

The nurses were given orders to wash his burns three
times a day, which they did not do. . . . Saturday Bob
decided to go home from the hospital. The nurses had
told him that they were just too busy to bother with his
burns.

So, fate stepped in to change everything. The doctors
had said that Bob had first-, second-, and third-degree
burns on his arms and hands. On Saturday morning we
decided to give him 600 IU of d-alpha tocopherol orally
and with one small batch of neosporin, we mixed 400 IU
vitamin E, stirred it all up and applied it to the burned
areas. The surgeon also prescribed antibiotic pills.

Bob saw the plastic surgeon Monday, and the doctor
told him that his fingers would be stiff, but Bob moved
them, and closed his fingers making a fist. The doctor
was amazed. I had asked Bob not to tell the doctor about

the E. He went to the doctor's office every other day, and the doctor could not believe what he saw. So Bob couldn't keep the secret any longer and told him of the vitamin E. Would you believe the doctor's answer? "It hasn't been clinically proven to me." Bob, in turn, asked him just how much proof he needs.

Bob didn't need the plastic surgery, and by May 21, hair was starting to grow out on the worst part of the burn on his lower arm. Between May 21 and 31, the doctors stopped all antibiotics, as his arm became fiery red. He also told Bob to use absolutely nothing on the burns. So, since I am not a doctor, Bob took his advice. By the time I found out about it, the skin had started to have tiny cracks, so I again persuaded Bob to start the E, both by mouth and by applying the oil from the capsules onto the burns every day.

There is still a discoloration on his arm, but if I can get him to continue to put E salve on his arm, let's hope, in time, the discoloration will disappear. What do you think, Doctor?

In the beginning Bob was told that he would be out of work for at least six months. He has been back to work since the second week of June (4½ weeks). Not bad! . . .

### Phlebitis

It has been at least four years since we last saw you as your patients. . . .

. . . My mother is now almost eighty-seven and she has had no phlebitis recurrences, except four years ago when my father died. It was a large lump in the inner thigh near the groin (inflammation covered an area about the size of a saucer) and we treated it by doubling her E, i.e., to 2,400 a day. In five days the inflammation was gone and the lump disappeared a few days thereafter. . . .

I am a thrombophlebitis case who accidentally became aware of your experiences with this condition through a friend of mine. I read your book, and was quite impressed with the chapter dealing with my condition. I have been hospitalized three times since April 1970, and have been on an anticoagulant since that time. My last stay in the hospital was for five weeks in December 1970, and January 1971, where I had exploratory surgery to see if I had any diseased organs. I was given a clean bill of health as far as having any diseased organs, however, my doctors could not determine what is causing the phlebitis to reoccur.

I had my local doctor read your chapter on phlebitis. He, too, was impressed and read the entire book. In checking with people at the university and a vascular specialist, he has not found anyone in this area who is overly impressed with the use of vitamin E for my condition.

I was determined to give it a trial and did so with the approval of my doctor. I took 600 IU of E per day for a period of about two weeks, then increased it to 1,200 IU per day for about two weeks. After about the third week, I no longer experienced any swelling, pain, or clotting in my legs, and have had none since. . . .

———————————

Your book has been read with great interest. Personally, having had a phlebitis condition in both legs for a period of over twelve years, I was ready to give vitamin E its trial. After several hospitalizations and all the regular treatments, my legs were getting progressively worse.

I have been on a dosage of 1,800 IU of vitamin E for a period of three months now. Remarkedly, there is less pain, little or none of the hot spots, and very slight edema compared to much edema previously by noon every day.

All this while I have been under the care of an internist who is in charge of the heart station of one of the hospitals, and who is beginning to show great interest in my progress. He has asked me to get any literature available on vitamin E.

———————————

## Heart Attack

I am writing this letter as though addressing an old friend. We have never met, yet I consider you just that. We met in 1967 through Herbert Bailey's book: *Vitamin E: Your Key to a Healthy Heart*. Ironically, I had picked that book as a possible help to my father-in-law who had had a heart attack and hardening of the arteries. The book was (surprisingly) for me too, because I had just been released from the hospital. When our son was born, I developed severe thrombophlebitis. I was still in excruciating pain and on the anticoagulants. It was to take me two full years before I felt truly well.

By the time he reached the bottom of one bottle of "E's, Grandpa was doing yard work he had not done in the past twelve years. On vitamin E the excruciating pain was also gone from my legs. Of course, I have been taking E ever since, as well as giving it to my two children and husband.) We had experienced a miracle, thanks to you! . . .

. . . My local cardiologist is now using vitamin E, personally, and prescribing it for his heart patients. He is Chief of Medicine and a cardiologist for one of our local hospitals.

For over four years, I have been supplying him with all the books that were available about vitamin E, and although he was courteous and promised to read them, he never expressed any opinion until recently when he told me that he is using vitamin E. He said the reason he is using it is because he has seen what it has done for me over the past four years, and he himself suffered a coronary two years ago. So we are making some progress in my town, because I am certain there will be other doctors who depend upon my doctor for diagnosis and he is the type of person who would not hesitate to at least recommend vitamin E.

———————————————•••••————————————

In 1970 my mother and dad had a heart attack, also

my mother-in-law, we were told, had a tired old heart and would die in three or four days.

All the doctors scoffed at the idea of using vitamin E.

We were using vitamin E anyway, but had feelings of anxiety. Were we really doing the right thing? Was it possible we were harming them?

I wrote you two letters and both times you answered by return mail.

All three people now are in great shape, no sign of any heart trouble of any kind. Mum is sixty-seven, Dad is seventy-two, and Mrs. Laird is eighty-three.

As Dad said to me, "Gee, Irene, it's great to be able to run for the bus."

Thank you, Dr. Shute, from us and all the others. . . .

———————————————

I wish to report the excellent results my mother had from vitamin E therapy. At the age of seventy-six she had slowly developed a heart condition which the local M.D. could not help. I had her take and continue large amounts of vitamin E, and now at the age of eighty she is in apparently good health, with no heart complaint. . . .

### Diabetes

. . . Harold, my husband, whom you met when you were a judge in the dog show here, has been taking vitamin E religiously since last August. He is a diabetic and you recommended E for him.

Well, his diet has not changed at all and since taking d-alpha tocopherol his blood sugar has decreased considerably from 165, two months later 162, three months later 130, then to 118, and last week his blood sugar was 100. He has been taking 750 IU daily. . . .

———————————————

. . . I have received great benefit by taking 600 IU of vitamin E daily. I have halved my intake of insulin. I also had a bad scalded foot which I treated with vitamin E ointment with success after six months nursing. . . .

In February of 1968, I developed a blood clot in my left eye. For four months with regular visits to an ophthalmologist, who said it might or it might not clear up, there was no improvement. I heard about vitamin E and decided to try it, starting with 600 IU. In three months the blood clot was gone.

I have increased the intake to 800 IU and seem to feel that my retinitis is diminishing. My insulin intake has been reduced from thirty-five to twenty-five units.

### Doctors Report on Vitamin E's Value

Thank you so much for your letter in reply to my enquiry regarding my wife's burned right forearm. We followed your advice . . . and have been using the vitamin E ointment as well as vitamin E orally.

All the second-degree burn area has now been healed for some time. Unfortunately, one part just below the elbow, of some fair size, was burned to about third-degree, and this of course is taking longer. However, the vitamin E ointment seems to be helping it greatly and we are much encouraged by the progress it has made.

———————————

I have had outstanding success with vitamin E therapy in my practice. Two years ago while snowmobiling in the Rockies, at an elevation of 9,000 feet, I experienced an acute shortness of breath. A year later, after months of vitamin E, I had less fatigue, greater exercise tolerance, and no shortness of breath.

My wife developed thrombophlebitis. On 1,200 IU of vitamin E, the phlebitis cleared up completely in four days.

Vitamin E is first choice in treating circulatory problems. It is an excellent prophylactic in the prevention of circulatory disease.

———————————

I want to congratulate you and thank you for the most important contribution, and so readable, your *Vitamin E for Ailing and Healthy Hearts*.

I have been on vitamin E for over thirty years, taking three 400 IU a day, one after each meal, and have had literally hundreds of patients on it.

In February, in Fort Lauderdale, a nice old lady of sixty-four years of age from Rochester, New York, came down there totally blind for six years; also a diabetic. She had a niece who was supposed to come every day and take her for a walk, but unfortunately the niece only came twice a week for ten minutes. The lady who ran the motel asked me if I would have a talk with the old lady. She was a little on the stout side and was very depressed because of the blindness.

I explained to her that I was not an "eye" man, but would like to put her on something. So I started her on vitamin E, 130 IU for three weeks, and told her then to step it up to 200 IU. On the twenty-eighth day I stopped by to see her and was told by the manager of the place, "You just missed Mrs. S———." I asked, "Has she gone home?" "Oh, no, she has just walked up to Britts." (Two long blocks.) He said she walks all over now and doesn't want anyone to go with her.

I was concerned, as there weren't sidewalks, and I asked him to tell the lady that I would be back the next day at 12:00 noon. When I got there I was told she didn't want me to go to her, that she would come to me. So I sat in the car till she came out with two little grandchildren, all smiles and stepping right along. She said, "I cannot see the fine print yet, but I am a completely new woman and my diabetes has almost cleared up. . . ." I have seen the miracles with vitamin E. I think you and your brother should be getting the Nobel Prize for popularizing vitamin E, undoubtedly the most important armament we have today for many conditions. . . .

———————————◆————————————

I am a colleague (psychiatrist), now in my seventy-second year and retired from practice. Some fifteen years ago I had some correspondence with you concerning vitamin E treatment for coronary trouble. On your recommendation I have continued to take, ever since and quite regularly, 800 IU a day. You may be pleased to hear that as far as the heart is concerned, my condition has remained satisfactory. . . .

---

I have been using vitamin E in my practice over twenty years and am well pleased with the results. I went on it years ago after a coronary thrombosis and except for some hypertension have been getting along well.

My wife developed asthma nine years ago and was kept on cortisone for two years with weight gain 135 to 185 pounds; a trip to Arizona relieved the asthma, but diabetes and fatty liver set in. She was on insulin, forty units daily, but vitamin E cut this to zero.

---

I wrote to you some time ago regarding the dosage of vitamin E for my angina, and although I have been unable to stop smoking as you advised me to do, I am much improved. I am still taking 3,200 IU a day, and have very few problems now, except for some shortness of breath with *undue* exertion. I tried cutting the intake down to 1,600 IU a day, but I simply feel better with the larger amount, so that is what I am using. I am well convinced that I owe the improvement to vitamin E. I have been prescribing it for a few patients.

. . . I feel that I might not be here today if it were not for your research, and I am most appreciative.

---

I am happy to report to you on Mr. R—— F——. This patient had severe coronary artery disease, and finally had a mammary artery implant, in late 1969. He was reevaluated in April 1970. The surgeon was somewhat disappointed, at that time, as he felt the results were not good. The patient continued to have quite severe angina and felt very poorly. On his own, a month or so later, he began taking vitamin E, 800 IU daily. Within two weeks, he began feeling much better, and within a month was able to return to work. . . .

I recently read your interesting book on vitamin E and looked up several of the references. Following this I treated a patient with transient cerebral ischemic attacks with vitamin E and obtained excellent results.

———————————•◆•———————————

. . . Several years ago I was fully convinced of the merits of your work. Nevertheless, my pharmacist—a much older man—scoffed at me (as did the O.M.A.). . . .

Regardless of medical opinion I prescribed vitamin E to many of my patients with rewarding results. One man in particular, age fifty-three, was told by his cardiologist a year ago last May that he could never work again. I suggested 400 IU vitamin E. This man is now working as a boiler installer and sometimes works as many as twelve hours a day. He has had no cardiac discomfort. . . .

———————————•◆•———————————

# Dr. Shute's Daughters Discuss the Value of Vitamin E in Their Work

*Like any father, I am proud of my children's accomplishments. However, I am doubly pleased that our two daughters have adopted careers in which they serve others. Moreover, their careers permit them to use what they have learned about vitamin E as they grew up in the atmosphere of my work. Both girls have applied the basic research on vitamin E to situations that have confronted them, and they have even found new areas of vitamin E's effectiveness that show promise.*

## Barbara Jane Shute Carnahan

*Barbara, our first born, owes her existence to vitamin E. The pregnancy which involved her was maintained with great difficulty, first with a potent wheat germ oil product, and later the first potent synthetic vitamin E—in heroic doses. Every day of her life Barbara has continued to take vitamin E, and it is due to vitamin E that she has maintained her two difficult pregnancies to their delightful conclusions. In turn, and under most unusual circumstances, vitamin E has proven of great value to both children. Barbara has also used vitamin E in her practice as a speech therapist in several cases.*

*W.E.S.*

# Hyperactive Children Can Learn

It was more by accident than by design that I found how vitamin E could be used effectively in my work.

A chance meeting between my father and one of my patients, a hyperactive boy with a severe speech problem, led me to realize that such children, in spite of learning problems, have a normal capacity to learn, and can be returned to the school system and grow up to be normal, happy members of society.

Let me start at the beginning: When we first moved to Delta, B.C. there was no speech therapist in the school district, and yet there was a very obvious need for this special service. I was anxious to work but felt I could not leave my home because of my newborn son. The school superintendent very graciously allowed me to do speech therapy in my house. This proved to be most successful. Since parental involvement, understanding, and responsibility help to speed progress, I have always insisted that one parent be with the child during therapy to insure his or her understanding of the child's case and my plan of work.

One of my first cases was T—— S——, a kindergartner referred to me by his teacher because his speech was virtually unintelligible. When I first examined him in April, the chances were very poor that his articulation and language would be acceptable by fall, when he was to enter Grade I. He had many sound substitutions, very weak auditory perceptual skills, and immature language patterns. He also seemed immature in his behavior and his attention span for listening was abnormally short.

T—— S—— received speech therapy once weekly and had homework to do every night. Teaching was very difficult due to his restlessness and short attention span. Nevertheless, T—— progressed rapidly. By the beginning of the summer, his articulation, language patterns, and auditory perceptual skills had improved to within normal limits. But we continued speech therapy into the summer because carry-over of the normal articulation and language patterns into spontaneous conversation was poor. Also, I wanted to make sure this boy would be able to survive Grade I both socially and academically. To this end, I was attempting to teach T—— the phonics he would need for the first session of school. Clearly, he had the ability to learn new skills and to use them appropriately, but his hyperactivity made it slow going.

T——'s mother, a nurse, found him increasingly difficult to handle at home. However, she refused to administer tranquilizers to reduce T——'s hyperactivity because they brought fresh difficulties, and the medication only masked the problem without solving it.

After a particularly frustrating session, I decided to release T—— for a short holiday before resuming therapy again at school. As he left my therapy room to go to the car, he left a path of littered toys, rearranged furniture, and a howling dog before his mother and I could physically restrain him. I was very upset at this display for I knew that with such behavior this boy could never adapt to the regular school system in spite of his good intellect.

My father happened to be visiting, and on impulse I introduced him to the boy and his mother. I asked if he had any ideas on how to reduce T——'s hyperactivity. He suggested that the boy be given 800 IU of vitamin E a day, and nothing else in the way of drugs, since any other medication could cloud the effect the vitamin E might have. His mother would have tried anything, I am sure, and readily agreed.

The first month of school passed before I was able to recheck T——. When I did, I was very surprised. His teacher reported that T——'s behavior in the classroom and in the school boundaries was within normal limits for his age. He was doing the same classwork as the rest of the children in Grade I, and progressing at normal speed. Furthermore, he was receiving no special attention for any learning problems. When I rechecked him, his articulation and language patterns were indeed within normal limits in spontaneous conversation.

I called his mother and she confirmed the same behavior results in the home situation. I did not need to see T—— again that year, nor has he needed speech therapy since. T—— is now in Grade III. His behavior is not a problem, but like all children with an auditory learning weakness, reading, phonics, and language arts do not come to him readily. However, because of his intellectual ability, he can cope with a regular school program. T—— is still an active boy, more so than his brothers. Vitamin E does not change the personality of a child nor does it "dope" him or her into passiveness, as do tranquilizers.

### Results and Reduced Dosage

At one time, his mother cut down T——'s vitamin E dosage to 400 IU a day and found that he immediately became more active, though not as uncontrollable as before. She put him back on 800 IU a day and not only did he calm down, but his school work improved immediately.

T——'s mother was so happy with his improvement that she started her other two children on 800 IU of vitamin E a day. The daughter suffered from eczema, and the ten-year-old son was troubled with continuing enuresis that persisted in spite of trying all known devices and medications. The daughter's eczema improved, though it did not disappear. The son's bed-wetting stopped completely within two days.

Not too long afterwards the mother was diagnosed as a diabetic and she was hospitalized to establish control of her diabetes. During this time the children became careless about taking their vitamin E. The daughter's eczema became worse and the son began to wet the bed again. When the mother was able to get the children back on vitamin E the son had no further problem with bed-wetting.

Several months later I had another opportunity to use vitamin E in my work.

I first met B—— L—— in the spring of his kindergarten year. He had a moderately severe articulation problem and was a very boisterous, clumsy boy with a booming voice. His mother, a quiet, diminutive lady, found it difficult to cope with her son. Yet, during speech therapy he cooperated willingly, his attention span was good, and he learned rapidly. As a result, though his articulation was still immature, it was good enough for me to discharge him in June of that year. He was rechecked in the early fall, and his articulation was still within normal limits for his age, so I decided that additional speech therapy was unnecessary.

In January, after the time of teacher interviews and report cards, his mother telephoned me to ask if B—— L—— could start working with me again. His mother was worried to the point of tears because her son was about to fail Grade I, but speech was not the main problem. According to the teacher, the boy's attention span was very short; he didn't finish any of his seat-work assignments; he was easily frustrated, and would talk out loud and create a commotion when he didn't succeed, or when he found the work too difficult. Yet the teacher was sure that B—— L—— had the ability to cope with Grade I if his work habits could be improved sufficiently.

The teacher was planning to put him on a modified primary program where he would be under less pressure, in the hope that his behavior might calm down.

We resumed therapy with the object of making B—— L——'s reading and written work better and quicker by strengthening auditory perceptual and phonic skills. In that way I thought he would be better able to cope in the classroom.

### Stretching the Attention Span

At the first session B—— L—— was a very tense, unhappy boy. He did not want to attempt anything new, he would break into tears when he didn't succeed immediately, and he was unable to sit still or attend to one activity for any length of time. His mother felt that this problem had become worse since he started Grade I. Boisterousness seemed acceptable in kindergarten because there were many opportunities to play energy-consuming physical games, and because school sessions were short. But with Grade I there was less opportunity to expend his energy. In fact B—— was expected to sit for long periods of time and do seat-work without any undue activity, and to absorb new material aurally (which means quietly).

After four months of this, B—— L—— had become the boy I have just described. However, his work had slipped just a little. After working on a one-to-one basis with his mother and with me, he was soon able to do the work that his class-mates were doing. Nevertheless, complaints about his behavior and his work habits in the classroom kept coming home. In desperation I suggested that this mother try giving her son 800 IU of vitamin E daily. She was only too willing.

I indicated to her that within ten to fourteen days there should be some improvement, if the vitamin E were going to work at all. Exactly ten days later the teacher very happily reported to Mr. L—— that this was the first day B—— L—— had completed his work and was able to attend the lessons calmly. B—— L——'s behavior was not a problem in the classroom for the rest of the year. His work habits and his work improved enough to enable him to pass into the regular Grade II.

The following October when I talked to this boy's Grade II teacher about his progress and his behavior, she reported that he was no problem and was doing well academically.

B.L. is now in Grade III and doing well. In fact, he is in the top one-third of his class. I must mention that he is still a rather boisterous boy who needs to run off a lot of energy. He has not changed in that way. He is still a worrier; he likes to win and to succeed and has a low frustration level. However, he not only copes in the regular classroom situation, but is able to stay in the top one-third of his class.

Incidentally, he is no longer taking vitamin E. Last Christmas his mother took him off it because "it didn't seem to be making any difference in his behavior." He is one of the fortunate ones whose behavior did not revert, or has not yet reverted, to its former state.

B—— A—— was first referred to me at the end of Grade I because of a mild articulation problem that had not corrected itself during the school year. With weekly speech therapy his articulation rapidly improved and was soon completely normal. However, I continued to see B—— for therapy during the summer because of a severe auditory perceptual problem and resulting learning disability.

B—— had trouble trying to learn through listening. As a result, he had not completed the required language arts, reading, or phonic skills of Grade I. Yet, he had enough strengths not to be failed outright. So he was placed on the modified primary program.

## Coping Through Bad Behavior

As part of the auditory learning problem, B—— was not able to pay attention during oral teaching for long periods of time or to remember oral instructions well. This led to many reprimands from the teacher. In response, B—— was learning to cope and compensate for his problems in learning through physical outlets. He was good at pulling pranks, fighting to defend himself, and getting into mischief. In other words, he was fast becoming a behavior problem at school and out of school.

Let me point out at this time that B——'s behavior was somewhat different than the two other cases previously mentioned. Although each one needed a lot of physical activity, the behavior of the first boy (T—— S——) can be considered a loss of control; the second boy (B—— L——) had his breakdown in response to pressure, while B—— A——'s was purposeful, intended to draw attention away from his failures academically. Like the other two boys, B—— desperately wanted to learn, wanted to be like his classmates, and was a tireless, hard worker. Under this aggressive front, he was a kind, considerate, gentle, sensitive, and frightened boy.

All of us worked hard that summer and fall of the second

year of school to keep B—— learning at the same rate as the others. In spite of all our work, progress, although steady, was ever so slow and B—— was fast falling behind his class-mates. Also his behavior in the classroom was rapidly de-teriorating. He was so disruptive that he had to be isolated in order that others, as well as himself, could get the required work finished.

It was at that time that his mother, a good friend and neighbor of the mother of B—— L——, learned that B—— L—— was taking vitamin E for his behavior problems at school and that he was doing well. So, B——'s mother asked me one day in March whether it was all right to give B—— the same. B—— was placed on 800 IU of vitamin E daily.

Unlike the other two hyperactive boys, there was no dra-matic change in behavior. Instead, B——'s ability to remem-ber, to absorb new learning, to use old and new learning appropriately, improved by leaps and bounds. And as his school work improved, his disruptive behavior in the classroom and on the playgrounds gradually lessened. He started to catch up to his classmates academically. His teacher was very pleased with his progress, so much so that she considered placing B—— in a regular Grade III class the next year. She and I both felt that B—— could now function without my therapy, with just special education in the school.

I released B—— from therapy that June but advised that he continue to have some special help in the school for his learn-ing disability and that he continue taking 800 IU of vitamin E daily.

In spite of this advice, I discovered that his mother discon-tinued his vitamin E during the following summer because, as she explained, she "couldn't see any real change in his be-havior."

*W.E.S. interjects here: This illustrates two of the problems in this case caused by the peculiarities of vitamin E therapy. In some medical problems vitamin E works in a matter of hours, or in a few days. But in most types of heart disease, improvement may begin to show in as little as ten days but will not be fully apparent for four, five, or six weeks. The time element can vary widely in many other types of abnormality for which vitamin E is a useful treatment. In the case of T—— S——'s brother, his enuresis cleared up in two days. In B—— A——'s case the effect was on behavior due to his inability to remember, to absorb new learning, to use old and new learning, and as a result his school work improved and his disruptive behavior in the classroom and on the playgrounds, lessened gradually. This was because he was sufficiently successful with his school work and didn't need to compensate or react with antisocial behavior. Now witness what happened when his mother discontinued the vitamin E.*

B—— is now in the fourth year of the four-year modified primary program. He is doing very poorly academically, especially in the language arts reading program. He is far behind his classmates. Although he will go into the regular Grade IV next year, he can barely read or do the seatwork of Grade II. He is a behavior problem in the classroom. He has trouble learning the classroom routines and abiding by the rules of the teacher.

Right now, B—— A—— is still trying and still working hard. But for all his efforts and the efforts of the special education teacher, he is making little progress. He has earned the reputation around the neighborhood as a "troublemaker." B—— A——'s parents are very concerned and anxious about his future. I am too.

My last case is perhaps the most interesting, as it concerns the use of vitamin E in the fields of speech and language therapy. Hitherto I had used vitamin E only with boys, only for hyperactivity, only indirectly as an aid to the actual speech therapy. But in J—— K——, a very withdrawn, passive girl, 800 IU of vitamin E daily was aimed directly at an auditory learning and language problem and an apparent miracle was achieved.

J—— K—— was referred to me in June of her Grade I year. I was a "last resort." This little girl was having immense learning difficulties. The parents were extremely concerned as was the school system, for J—— was fast becoming an "emotional wreck." The problem was: nobody quite knew what the problem was.

Academically, J—— K——'s learning was erratic, some skills had been acquired, others had not. For example, she was able to read only single words, could not apply phonics or do the seatwork, nor could she follow or understand the group lessons.

Emotionally, she was barely coping. She was ill before school, afraid and confused by the multitude of children in the school halls and on the playground, and easily distracted in the classroom. J—— had trouble making friends and feeling that she was part of the group. She was withdrawn and refused to participate in class activities. Most of these behavioral difficulties disappeared at home.

The school tested J—— and found her to be developmentally immature. They then placed her back in a kindergarten class and, emotionally, she fell to pieces altogether. The parents had objected to this arrangement from the start because J——'s younger brother was in kindergarten and they felt that this situation might be harmful.

The school then tried giving J—— special education every day to bring her reading skills to Grade I level. But this failed too, for J—— was fearful of leaving the classroom, of being different, of not getting her work done when she returned to the classroom. The school and the parents were at odds with each other: the parents were convinced that J—— had the ability; the school felt that J—— was too immature for Grade I.

Finally, after a very bad Easter report card, the parents went to the school district superintendent and asked for further testing of J—— by the school district psychologist. This was done and her tests indicated poor verbal and language functioning. For this reason J—— was referred to me for therapy, even though she had no speech problem.

My first encounter with J—— was very painful for her and her mother. J—— would not willingly leave the car to see me. She was very fearful and, in fact, had been ill that morning in anticipation of our meeting. But once inside, she calmed down considerably and cooperated fully.

In the next few sessions, it became readily apparent that J—— had a severe auditory learning disability. But her visual perceptual and motor skills were also weak and so there was no strong alternative sensory approach to learning. On the other hand, J—— had many strengths including a strong desire to learn, the ability to stick with difficult tasks, and a willingness to work long and hard if success were apparent. There were also many strengths in the family that were very much in J——'s favor, such as tremendous support, understanding, compassion, and a belief in her.

At the onset of therapy, our goals were to strengthen J——'s auditory perceptual and language skills, and apply these skills to the Grade I language arts and phonics program. At the end of the summer, J—— would be retested to see what progress she had made and in what areas. Then it would be decided where J—— was to be placed in school. The parents did not want J—— to fail Grade I or be put on the modified program. And the school did not see how J—— could possibly enter Grade II.

Therapy was started immediately on a once-weekly basis with homework assignments to be carried out with her mother every day. J—— was now working hard and willingly.

But in spite of all our organized, well-planned, well-varied therapy sessions and homework assignments, progress was slow and erratic, and far below expectations.

In desperation, I suggested to Mrs. K—— that she try J—— on 800 IU of vitamin E daily. The mother was very much against this idea since, as she expressed it, she did not believe in flagrant unprofessional use of "drugs" for problems that could be resolved with hard work. I suggested that she consult her doctor for his opinion on whether such a dosage of this vitamin might harm J——. Fortunately, in spite of her initial objections, by the following week she had put J——

on the suggested dose of vitamin E and was giving it to her faithfully.

### Improvement in Ten Days

Within the following ten days there were some changes in J——'s learning pattern. The most remarkable and necessary of these from my point of view, was her ability to absorb new learning and retain it, and use it appropriately in different situations. From this time on, progress was steady, continuous, and rapid. By the end of summer, we had covered all the basic skills of Grade I as concerns the language arts, reading, and phonic program. Incidentally, I did not work on changing the atypical behavior patterns J—— had shown at school and, to a lesser degree, at home. They are understandable reactions and ways of coping with a severe auditory disability. However, all but one gradually disappeared as J——'s auditory perceptual skills grew stronger. We did have to do some desensitization therapy to increase auditory attention in a noisy environment.

September came and because of hard work and remarkable progress during the summer, J—— was placed in a regular Grade II class. Both the family and I were apprehensive as to J——'s reactions to school that first week. However, she was not only eager to start but for the first time ever, insisted on going by herself without her mother. She immediately settled into the classroom and became a participating, contributing, normal member.

During the fall term, therapy was continued on a once-weekly basis. We now incorporated the Grade II language arts and phonics program into our therapy sessions. At the end of the term J——'s reports indicated that her behavior, participation, and effort in class were excellent, and there was steady progress in her learning and achievements. However, at the next therapy session that J——'s behavior had de-indicated that J—— was still not up to the regular Grade II level and that the parents should understand that she might have to repeat or be put on the modified primary program in June.

We continued therapy as before during the winter term until the end of March. J—— continued to work hard, was happy and content; she was getting so she didn't like to miss school to come to me for therapy, and even more important was gaining some insight into her problems. When her Easter report came out her mother rushed over to me with tears in her eyes. J—— was doing regular Grade II work, keeping up to her classmates on a low-average level, and was definitely going to pass into a regular Grade III in June.

J—— is now in a normal Grade III class and is working well at an average level. She continues to take 800 IU of vitamin E daily.

It is interesting to note that when J—— was doing well, I suggested to her mother that she take J—— off vitamin E for awhile to see what happened. Her mother refused to even consider the idea now that J—— was a "normal, happy child." It is also interesting that when she forgot to give J—— her vitamin E for a couple of days in a row, it was obvious at the next therapy session that J——'s behavior had deteriorated; she had trouble remembering and nothing new could be introduced into the lesson that day.

In summary, I have used vitamin E in only the last three years of my ten-year practice. I used it only in cases where there was no improvement in spite of everything that could be done for the child, and I obtained remarkable results. Vitamin E did work amazingly well for hyperactivity, but even more surprising, it improved the child's ability to learn through a defective or damaged sensory channel. Think of all the hope there is for children who have learning disabilities, yet good minds, and you will be as excited about this discovery as I am.

### Answering Some Common Questions

Let me close the therapy discussion by answering some of the questions that the parents have asked me about the use of vitamin E.

Q. Is vitamin E dangerous in such a large dose (800 IU) to the children?

A. No.

Q. Are there any side effects to such a large dose?

A. None, unless a child is allergic to the substance and such allergies are exceedingly rare. There are three forms of vitamin E, so even if a child is allergic to one, it is unlikely that the child will be allergic to all three.

Q. Does vitamin E accumulate in the body, so that it might, at some future time, cause harm?

A. No. Vitamin E is absolutely essential to the normal function of every cell in the body and fortunately, some is stored in all organs and in fatty tissue. However, at the dosage level used in these patients, the excess over minimum body needs is rapidly excreted in as little as three days.

You will remember that the brother of T—— S——, the first patient I described, stopped bed-wetting in two days, but when he became careless with his vitamin E during the mother's hospitalization, he began to wet again. And when J——, the little girl, missed two days of vitamin E, her ability to learn and retain decreased markedly. This emphasizes the importance of continuous, daily intake at the effective level. Once a patient shows improvement, it will continue gradually, often for many months. The patient who is careless will have ups and downs, and after as little as three days without E, may revert to his or her former state.

Q. Is vitamin E a drug?

A. No. It is a nutrient essential to normal body functions.

Q. How long will the child have to take vitamin E?

A. I have found that after getting good results parents tend to become careless or assume that the child no longer needs the supplementary vitamin E. The parents think vitamin E is like an antibiotic; once the symptoms are gone, they no longer need to continue the dosage. Of course, this is not so and the children tend to revert to their learning problems and behavioral difficulties when vitamin E support is removed.


*W.E.S. comments: These are the first reports I know of on the response of hyperkinetic (hyperactive) children to mega-*

*vitamin E therapy. More significant perhaps is the response to vitamin E therapy of children with a defective or damaged sensory channel.*

*Any person aware of the deterioration of our society with its increase of hyperkinetic children with learning disabilities from about 2 percent in the average school population to a figure of 20 percent to 25 percent, and in some areas as much as 40 percent in some schools, must find Barbara's report significant and stimulating. Such children become school drop-outs at best, and since they often cannot hold a job, may well swell the ranks of juvenile delinquents.*

I have found it particularly frustrating when parents comment that there has been "no change in behavior." Vitamin E does not change the basic personality of a child. This is as it should be. Because the parents have become familiar with the use of drugs which tranquilize the child, they expect the same change when vitamin E is given. What I am striving for is a change in the ability to learn, which occurs slowly but steadily; it is a very subtle change and the most wonderful change of all. It does not happen with tranquilizers or with any other treatment. I cannot understand why the parents do not appreciate this important distinction.

### Erin

Of course, to my mind, the best of my part in this book is about my daughter Erin, now just two years old. The story of Erin and vitamin E really began before her birth. In the very first month of my pregnancy with her, I started to bleed, not heavily, but enough to know that something was not right. I was then on 800 IU of vitamin E a day. I went to my obstetrician very much concerned, and after a thorough examination, I was told that there was only a 50 percent chance of my carrying this baby to term. Instead of just doing nothing, I doubled my dose of vitamin E to 1,600 IU a day on my own. The very next day I stopped bleeding and eight months later, delivered by natural childbirth, a beautiful eight-pound, four-ounce girl.

Erin is my constant ray of sunshine, but she is so curious, so quick, and she does get into things. In December, just before her first birthday, she tried a mouthful of the dog's raw hamburger, and as a result of that she spent four days in the hospital with salmonella poisoning. Just after her first birthday, on a Sunday afternoon, her quick little fingers grabbed a handful of popcorn from the bowl that the rest of us were enjoying. Since popcorn is high on the list of hard foods that babies should not have (they tend to inhale such foods into their lungs) we swiftly took most of the popcorn away from our daughter.

That night, Erin's breathing started to get a little loud, a little hoarse. Thinking that she was coming down with a good cold, I put her to bed with a dose of some children's cough medicine. The next morning Erin indeed seemed to have developed a chest cold as indicated by her loud wheezy breathing. By Wednesday, I had become alarmed for each day her wheezing got louder, and now she was breathing heavily and with effort.

At the doctor's the next day, Erin was given an x ray along with a very thorough examination, to make sure that nothing was in her lungs. The x ray was clear, and since her lungs seemed clear by listening, it was thought that she had a severe case of croup. She was sent home on Amphycilin.

The following Monday I was back at the doctor's, for Erin's breathing had not improved on the medication; in fact, it was becoming worse. At this appointment, Erin's pediatrician listened to her chest for a considerable time, and then called in his partner to confirm his suspicions. There was very little air getting into the right lung. Because of Erin's popcorn-eating, it was assumed that there was a piece of popcorn in her lung even though the x ray had seemed clear. We were sent to a very competent pediatric surgeon that afternoon, and by evening Erin was in the hospital. She was given a bronchoscopy the next day. The surgeon told us that he had removed a lot of mucus, and what he thought were tiny particles of popcorn.

Erin's recovery that week was slow, ever so slow, slower than normal. Her breathing was still wheezy though less so, and she was in a tent for part of the day and all night to help her breathing. She was started on twice-daily sessions of physiotherapy because she had developed fluid in the lower lobe of her lung. However, by the following Tuesday she was home from the hospital since her breathing seemed better. I was to continue physiotherapy twice a day.

After a day at home, it became apparent that something was still wrong, for Erin's wheezing was starting again, and by the time we went to the pediatrician's on Friday for a checkup, her breathing was as labored and noisy as before. Not only that, there was still little, if any, air getting into her right lung. She was readmitted to the hospital that afternoon for more tests and x rays.

My husband and I had an appointment with the pediatrician Monday afternoon to discuss the problem and what was going to be done. Unfortunately, he could offer no definite solution. They would have to continue testing, and we were to prepare ourselves for the possibility of cystic fibrosis, TB, and other uncommon lung ailments. I cried and cried.

### More Surgery Reveals Problems

The following afternoon Erin went into surgery again. This time when the surgeon came out of the operating room he told us that he had found the problem. There was an area of infection in the bronchus leading into the right lung that had increased in size since the last bronchoscopy, and was blocking off the air into the lung. He thought it was TB, but to be sure he had taken a biopsy specimen for microscopic examination and for a culture.

It is interesting to note at this point that a TB test is one of the several routine tests that are given to all children upon entering the hospital. But Erin was first admitted during the intern's strike in the Province, so she did not receive this, or some of the other routine tests.

The rest of the week Erin was given numerous tests. The cystic fibrosis proved negative but the TB test on her arm was very positive. A TB and lung specialist was called into the case. He spent the rest of the week doing more tests. A specific diagnosis was difficult since her condition was not characteristic of human tuberculosis, even though her tuberculin test was strongly positive. Instead, he thought it must be another type of infection, fortunately very rare, called avian tuberculosis which unfortunately also shows a positive tuberculin test. On further examination Erin showed a positive reaction to the specific test for this rare infection.

Erin was discharged a week after the second bronchoscopy. At this time her breathing was almost normal during the daytime, but after getting up from her nap she would cough and wheeze ever so slightly for awhile.

During all this testing and while Erin was in the hospital, I had given her no vitamin E. However, when we telephoned Daddy about Erin's problem he advised us to start Erin on 800 IU of vitamin E a day since he had cured a patient suffering from extensive tuberculosis with vitamin E many years before. So, as soon as she was out of the hospital, as well as the regular medication for tuberculosis, she was given 800 IU of vitamin E in pill form, swallowed as she took her bottle. Erin continued to improve rapidly. Her breathing became normal in about a month's time; she started to eat better, she became an active, curious girlie again. But there was still only 50 to 60 percent of the air getting into the right lung. She was given a checkup every two weeks.

Two months later, the results of the culture came back. The laboratory had taken extra time and precaution on Erin's culture because of her age. The results for the normal TB were negative. It was proven that Erin had a very rare form of TB called avian TB or atypical microbacteria—a TB-like disease, very rare, found in the lower mainland of British Columbia, Canada. They also found out that the disease was resistant to the TB drugs. In fact, there are no known drugs to cure it. Therefore, following a conference of all the specialists involved with Erin's illness, she was taken off all drugs. We were advised that she should continue regular bimonthly checkups, that she receive an x ray every two months or so and have a bronchoscopy about twice a year. Very little is known about the disease but they do know that it is self-limiting; it is not contagious; it does not recur.

The only sinister detail about the disease is that it creates scar tissue as it dies. The pediatrician was especially cautioning about this aspect. There was a possibility that the scar tissue could close off the lung again, and if left untreated, could mean a collapsed and permanently damaged lung, which may result in partial resection of one or more lobes. Unfortunately, to his knowledge, there was no way of helping or of preventing this.

Summer came and went and Erin grew strong, healthy, and happy. Our checkups became less frequent because Erin was so well, and because there was gradually more and more air getting into her lung. By the end of September, the time had come for Erin to have more x rays and to enter the hospital for a bronchoscopy. Since Erin was so well and since there was no medical necessity for further hospitalization, I refused all of these tests.

In December, Erin was rechecked by the surgeon who performed the bronchoscopies. He examined her ever so thoroughly and found her to be normal; i.e. her lung was clear—there was the same amount of air going into both lungs.

By February, a year after Erin was first hospitalized, our pediatrician found Erin to be in excellent health; growing normally and best of all, as far as he could tell without x rays, her right lung was functioning normally, and there was the normal amount of air going into the lung.

Erin is still on 800 IU of vitamin E a day, and will be for a very long time.

*W.E.S. comments: Vitamin E relaxes early scar tissue and prevents excessive scarring. The scars that are formed do not contract, so I was sure that Erin's bronchus would not be narrowed or obstructed. The contraction and narrowing that was present was obviously overcome by the 800 IU of vitamin E a day.*

**Plastic Surgery Avoided**

Another gratifying experience with vitamin E concerns my son. He was standing up on the front seat of the car when the car in front of me in the parking lot began to move forward, and then suddenly braked to a stop. To keep from hitting it, I put on my brakes suddenly and James, who was a year and a half old, was thrown forward, his head striking the rear-view mirror. A piece of skin, the size of a nickel, was gouged out of his forehead to one side of the mid-line.

The doctor's office was just across the street and when he saw it, he told me to get the piece of skin and perhaps he could sew it back on. I had to get the service station attendant to remove the mirror, and I carried the mirror, with its attached skin, back to the doctor. He washed the skin in saline, sewed it back on James' forehead, and covered it with a large dressing.

This dressing quickly became saturated at the edges with blood from the wound. I had been told not to disturb the dressing for a week, since the skin graft, if it had become stuck to the dressing, could easily be pulled off. He also told me that there was a good chance that the graft would not "take" since there was little blood supply in this area, and the patch was quite large.

My sister Karen urged me to soak the dressing off so I could apply vitamin E ointment to the area, and thus increase the chance that the skin which had been sewn back would "take." My dilemma was solved when my father suggested that I soak the bandage with vitamin E ointment so as to loosen the bandage from the underlying skin and allow its safe removal. As soon as this was accomplished I applied the vitamin E ointment liberally and kept the wound covered with it.

When I took James back to the doctor a week after the accident, to have the stitches removed, the doctor was very happy about its appearance although, at this time, the center of the graft was a bit discolored and appeared to be drying up. Also it was noted that the edges were reddened and looked as if the very edges of the graft might die out.

With the constant application of the ointment, both areas improved. The doctor at this stage said that James would certainly need plastic surgery later, to remove scar tissue and smooth down the area. He felt there would be a very noticeable and ugly scar.

I continued to apply the ointment for several months, faithfully every day, and I do it still whenever I remember. The scar is now flat and unnoticeable unless you know where to look, and look closely in a good light. The original wound was at the hair-line and hair is now growing normally in the upper portion of the grafted skin.

Vitamin E has been so useful in our family that there is a tube of the ointment in just about every room in the house. It should be in every home!

# Karen Kathleen Shute Berry

*Karen, our second born, also owes her existence to vitamin E. It was even more difficult for my wife to maintain the pregnancy which involved her, and when Karen was born she was not only an obviously toxic baby, but the placenta showed three large infarcts. Karen grew up to be an outstanding athlete. She is a Registered Nurse, and after a course at the University of British Columbia, is now a Public Health Nurse.*

*She is employed in a Public Health Unit and has directly and indirectly been responsible for introducing vitamin E to her friends and to people she meets in her "practice."*

# Philosophy Emphasizes Promotion of Health

The Public Health Nurses' philosophy emphasizes the promotion and maintenance of health, the prevention of disease and of disability, and the provision of comprehensive care of the sick and disabled in the community setting. So as a Public Health Nurse, I have had many opportunities to apply my knowledge of vitamin E therapy.

The medical profession has always been very conservative about initiating new techniques in therapy. You may remember the long struggles for the acceptance of insulin and penicillin by medical men. Similarly, although vitamin E therapy has been used successfully for thirty years, it is still labeled "controversial" by many doctors.

My medical training in the hospital for three years, and later in the University of British Columbia, have conditioned me to be conservative like most nurses in my work, so it has been difficult for me to break away from the norm. However, being so close to my father's amazing achievements has made it impossible for me to stand by while people suffer or even die when they might have been helped by vitamin E therapy.

As a nurse, I am not allowed to prescribe treatments. However, I can suggest to people that they investigate vitamin E treatment and I can provide them with the sources of information they need to do so.

In my work, I see a great number of ailments that are alleviated by vitamin E, ranging from relatively minor ones like diaper rash, to more serious problems such as crib-death syndrome, birth injuries, burns, and habitual miscarriages. How can one treatment be effective in so many ways? Remember, vitamin E is an antioxidant and functions to limit the need for oxygen in the tissues and organs of the body. This affects circulation in general and, in turn, affects the complete functioning of the body.

To illustrate the effectiveness of vitamin E let me describe several cases in my experience. The first deals with crib deaths or SIDS (Sudden Infant Death Syndrome). Some recent research suggests that crib deaths occur because of a lack of oxygen in the area of the brain that triggers the breathing reflex.

An apparently normal, healthy baby is put to bed; hours later, with no warning cry, the child is dead. Many suggested causes—suffocation, infections, allergic reactions—have been disproved. But research by Dr. Richard L. Naeye, at Pennsylvania State University's M.S. Hershey Medical Center, indicates that the SIDS babies are victims of a long-term shortage of oxygen. Previously, Dr. Alfred Steinschneider at Upstate Medical Center in Syracuse, New York, noted that two babies who later died of SIDS had frequently suffered long spells of nonbreathing. Then, in 1975, Dr. Naeye reported that the small arteries of the lungs of SIDS babies had an abnormal overgrowth of smooth-muscle fiber, a condition common in adults with chronic oxygen shortage ailments. Recently, he discovered that, in SIDS infants, the brown fat which coats babies' adrenal glands at birth (normally replaced within three to four months by white fat) is retained longer.

### Adequate Oxygen for Premature Babies

Classically, at least in our area of Canada, doctors are concerned about insuring adequate oxygen in these premature babies. Also, since many are anemic, doctors supply supplementary iron in the formula. However, since vitamin E and iron are antagonistic, this added iron cancels any vitamin E in the formula.

The basic formula, even without the added iron, probably contains corn oil with a large proportion of polyunsaturated fats, which adversely affects the vitamin E content. The premature infant then has whatever vitamin E he is born with depleted or removed nearly entirely by the polyunsaturated fats and the iron until he is discharged from the hospital.

My first report concerns a premature baby boy with poor oxygen supply to the vital respiratory center of the brain and, therefore, a candidate for crib death. Fortunately, the problem was recognized in time so that supplementary oxygen and artificial respiration kept him alive until he was discharged and could be treated with vitamin E—the substance which decreases oxygen need. The expected response to vitamin E therapy was obtained and the infant no longer needed additional oxygen or artificial respiration.

This baby boy was born six to eight weeks prematurely, with a birth weight of three pounds, eleven ounces. After forty-eight hours, the baby began to have spells of apnea, or temporary loss of breath. These continued to occur for 10 days, then stopped. When he was twenty-one days old, he aspirated some formula and suffered a cardiac arrest, after which the spells of apnea began again. He would go cyanotic (blue) and stimulation would not start his breathing again until oxygen was administered, and in some instances resuscitation was necessary. These spells became very frequent —up to twenty-one in a single day. Gradually, during the three months the infant was in the hospital, the spells occurred less often, usually only during a feeding and eventually, he was down to about four a day.

The baby finally came home using a cardiac monitor, which provided auditory monitoring of the heart beat and had an automatic alarm which would sound if the heart stopped. (Doctors learned that the baby's heart rate slowed at the onset of a spell of apnea.) At home, the iron was removed from the formula and vitamin E was begun: thirty IU a day for three weeks, with no real response. Vitamin E at sixty IU a day was given for the next week, and then ninety IU a day, and during the next month the baby suffered only three spells. For several months thereafter the monitor was removed except at night. Understandably, the mother was nervous and didn't want to take any chances.

After the spells had stopped entirely, and at my father's

suggestion, the baby's dosage was raised to 800 IU a day, a dosage he had used on many infants and young children before. He felt sure this amount would guarantee that the baby would never have another spell. One hundred mg. of vitamin C per day was added to the vitamin E since each enhances the other's properties.

Two other conditions occurred in this baby: first, he had two large raised strawberry birthmarks on his left forearm, one two and one half inches by two inches, and the other, three quarters of an inch square. Vitamin E ointment was applied to them several times a day. We expected that these would shrink, but to our surprise their color deepened. Then they began to lighten, starting at the center, and eventually assumed the color of the surrounding skin. The swelling diminished also, becoming, in essence, normal tissue.

Second, when this baby was tested before discharge from the hospital, he was found to have a lack of normal muscle tone. Because of this, he was behind in his task development. However, at eight months, his muscle tone had become normal and so had his development.

I have discussed this case with my father and asked him to comment. Here he is:

*This child illustrates two aspects of such cases. His mother had shown all the classical symptoms of a vitamin E-deficient pregnancy. At the beginning, she "spotted" sporadically. This was her first pregnancy and she did not know she was pregnant at this time. She had severe nausea for four months, and toward the end of her pregnancy, her face, feet, and hands were puffy. Then, too, the baby was born prematurely, six to eight weeks before term, and weighed three pounds, eleven ounces. This woman would almost certainly have avoided all these complications, and the baby might well have been carried to term had she been given vitamin E as soon as it was realized that she was spotting because she was pregnant. Her nausea and vomiting could have been arrested with vitamin E or with male sex hormone. Both counteract the effects of hyperestrogenemia, the cause of the nausea and vomiting.*

*The mother very likely also suffers from hypothyroidism since these are the people who have excessive estrogen and develop these problems.*

*The original work in this field was done by my older brother, Evan, and he and my younger brother have had success in controlling these conditions in their obstetrical practices. Their work is well documented, thoroughly confirmed and known world-wide.*

*It is probable, therefore, that an E-deficient mother gave birth to an E-deficient child.*

*The matter of anemia in premature infants, and its treatment, has been the subject of several papers, notably those of Ritchie and his group as reported in the* New England Journal of Medicine, *(279, No. 22, 1185-1190, 1968) and Oski and Barnes in the* Journal of Pediatrics *(70:211, 1967.) The former described the anemia in premature infants as being a vitamin E deficiency syndrome, and described its correction by vitamin E, but only when iron and polyunsaturated fats are removed from the diet. This infant illustrates the time element stressed in the Ritchie paper, that after the removal of the iron and unsaturated fats, it still takes up to ten days for results to start to appear, with a return to normal in most cases by four weeks. They used 100 IU daily in the treatment of their patients and this child then responded on approximately that dosage level, as could have been anticipated.*

*The response of the birthmark to vitamin E is the second in our experience. The first reported was in the sister of a doctor whose birthmark began to disappear around its border with the use of vitamin E applied locally in the form of an ointment.*

Another case involved a sixty-eight-year-old woman troubled with a blood clot in her right leg. It was quite unbearable at times as she was very active and on her feet almost all day long. She happened to rent an apartment to me and I told her about the value of vitamin E in such cases. She started vitamin E at 800 IU per day and in less than eight days the ache and fatigue had left her completely. She really was amazed at the results.

After several months she ran out of vitamin E and two or three days later the old trouble returned. This was at least a good test, for the lady was now convinced that she must take it regularly. She started again and was completely relieved once more.

## Diabetic Gangrene Responds to Vitamin E

When I was transferred to another Public Health Unit in British Columbia, among the nurses I met there was a diabetic who was recovering with the help of vitamin E from a recent brush with diabetic gangrene of the toe. I suggested to her that her dosage was too small and should really be doubled. Her history, as she wrote it herself, follows:

> I had been on 400 IU vitamin E and had been able to cut down some on the insulin. Then when the toe came up I increased to 800 IU. The toe was really slow healing—three months. When it healed I came back to work and here was Karen who told me I should be on 1,600 IU. So then I started decreasing the insulin gradually until I was stabilized on half of my previous dosage and feeling great. I managed to get by many cuts and scrapes on my legs and feet with no infection. Before taking vitamin E my usual time necessary to heal an infection on my leg or foot was three or four months. Now, it takes about a week and a half.

Last spring, this nurse suffered a fracture of the foot on her "bad side" and a cast involving leg and foot was necessary. This was, of course, a hazardous necessity since any injury from the cast—a pressure sore due to swelling inside the cast or chaffing—could be dangerous, especially in that leg. Two sores did develop on the top side of the foot just behind the base of the toes and when the cast came off they were raw and oozing serum, but these healed promptly without incident. This leg is now normal in color and pulsations in the supplying arteries are normal or nearly so.

Of course with my sister Barbara living just minutes away,

I knew about her experiences with hyperactive children and vitamin E. A year or so ago I encountered a similar case and was able to contribute to the child's recovery.

This was the mother's first pregnancy. She showed albuminuria throughout the whole pregnancy and although the baby was full term, he weighed only four pounds, five ounces and was a very long and lean baby, but apparently normal and bright. He was home for three weeks and then developed a pyloric stenosis, which was relieved surgically.

While in the hospital after delivery and again during surgery, he was a very "good baby," but when sent home after the operation, the physician instructed his mother to feed him hourly with a formula heavy in sugar until he was three months old. During this period the baby was easily distracted from nursing by noise. He would stop and could be restarted only with difficulty. He did not sleep well, only in catnaps if disturbed by noise.

At five months he was started on solids. He didn't like milk so ate only meat and vegetables. During the next four months he was a very good, quiet baby. However, at nine months he became extremely constipated and his doctor put him on brown sugar, one teaspoon in five or six ounces of water, two or three times a day, plus strained baby fruit. He rapidly became quite erratic in behavior, a very nervous child, high-strung, jittery, and unable to cope with any change in routine. For example, he was hysterical for three days because his father instead of his mother went into his bedroom to get him up.

### Four-Year-Old Unwelcome at Grandma's House

I met the mother when the boy was aged four and readying for school. The boy's grandmother had refused for some time to have the boy in her home because he was so disruptive. I told them both about Barbara's success with vitamin E in treating hyperactive children. They decided to try it. On 600 IU a day of vitamin E (soon raised to 800 IU) the boy became calmer within three days. He was no longer getting "highs and lows," now ate mild snacks three or four times a day, and his sleeping improved.

During the previous two years he tossed and turned all night. The slightest noise outside woke him and usually he was up by 4:30 A.M., going through cupboards gobbling anything sweet, often including handfuls of straight sugar. The change was dramatic. At night he lay quietly in bed and slept soundly.

Shortly after beginning vitamin E a playmate accidentally fractured this boy's collarbone. It healed completely in ten days. But surprisingly there was no traumatic reaction at all, no behavioral upset as a result of the stress of this accident.

All sources of sugar and all sources of artificial coloring and artificial flavoring were removed from the boy's diet. After four months on no sugar, no artificial flavoring or artificial coloring, and 800 IU of vitamin E, his progress at preschool was termed "fantastic." His teachers who tried to get an attention span of three minutes without success, now were able to hold his attention for over half an hour. Before, he could not be disciplined; now he was no longer a problem.

Another marked change was in the boy's speech. He did not start speaking until he was nearly three years old, and then he was "going so fast he was almost babbling." After treatment was initiated he began to speak more slowly and distinctly and his language now is almost normal. I am convinced that vitamin E played a major role in this child's personality change, though the dietary alterations undoubtedly influenced the final result.

The next case involves a girl two and one-half years old. According to the mother's reckoning, this infant was one month overdue. At birth she weighed three pounds, fourteen ounces. It was a transverse presentation, that is, the baby lay crosswise to the birth canal.

**Use of Paralyzed Arm Restored**

At birth the baby had complete paralysis of the left arm, and partial paralysis of the left side of the face. The arm was placed in a sling and remained so for the first three months since there was no motion whatsoever from the shoulder downwards.

When she was three months old, the parents took the baby to a noted neurologist who told them that the baby would never have any use or feeling in that arm.

At this point, I spoke to the mother about the possibility that vitamin E might help restore some use to the arm, and she then started to give the baby 100 IU of E a day. After three weeks, there was very slight but definite movement of the arm away from the body. The dosage of vitamin E was then raised to 300 IU a day and electrical stimulation of the muscles of the arm and forearm was begun, and continued for two months. Again, there was improvement with considerable movement extending now even to the fingers. Again the dosage of vitamin E was raised, to 800 IU a day, with a gradual return of feeling.

Improvement has continued steadily on 800 IU a day, and she now has all feeling, uses this hand, moves her arm well, but cannot straighten the elbow completely. She is regaining her wrist movements. She began physiotherapy three times a week and the doctor and the physiotherapist expect her to regain full use of the arm.

Another friend's husband has a case worth reporting. A year ago superficial phlebitis developed. He was treated with phenylbutazone which gave slight relief. Several weeks later, a specialist did a venogram and within an hour the patient developed severe, deep pain. He returned to the doctor who said that it was not caused by the procedure. A week later, the swelling in the leg was so severe and painful that ten days of hospitalization, with heparin every six hours, was ordered.

One week after his release from the hospital, the swelling behind the knee became so severe that he couldn't bend it and he had to be rehospitalized. Heparin every six hours and warfarin by mouth was again given. The warfarin was increased to thirty mg. a day. This hospitalization lasted for two weeks. After discharge, the patient had daily prothrombin (clotting) time taken with adjustment of the warfarin dosage as indicated. The average dose level at this time was approximately thirty mg. After five to six weeks on warfarin, the doctor told him he would "never be totally better."

At this point, the patient who had been urged by his wife to take vitamin E finally agreed to try it, although reluctantly. He would only take 200 to 400 IU a day, and continued the warfarin. After six weeks, he returned to the specialist who expressed amazement at his improvement. Shortly afterwards, he started bleeding from the bowel. His family doctor told him to stop the warfarin but the specialist urged that he continue it.

At his wife's insistence the patient raised his dosage of vitamin E to 800 IU a day. Five weeks after this bleeding episode he returned to the specialist who discontinued warfarin.

Here is an interesting sidelight to the story: At this visit, the specialist asked the patient if he had ever heard of alpha tocopherol, and suggested that he take 600 IU of it! Somewhat surprised, and without telling the doctor he had been taking vitamin E, the patient said, "Do you think that is enough?" The specialist said, "Put it this way, if all my patients for the last ten years had been taking 600 IU a day, I wouldn't have any patients." He also refused to prescribe vitamin E although he wanted the patient to take it, saying he couldn't *make* him take the vitamin E.

After this visit the patient read Dad's latest book. After reading this, he started taking 2,400 IU a day. The leg cleared up within three weeks. Then he reduced the dose to 1,600 IU a day and then to 800 IU. He had missed a total of seven months' work and his condition had worsened steadily while on his doctor's orthodox treatment, but cleared up almost completely with the vitamin E treatment.

# Index

# Index of Authors and Titles

No more reason

for

throat

to

thirst.

Halloween's

over.

It's

November

FIRST.

# 12:01 A.M.

## BY LEE BENNETT HOPKINS

No more reason

to

shudder,

shake,

shiver,

tremble,

quiver,

quake.

# Black Cat

BY NATASHA WING

Black cat

against a yellow moon

casts a blue shadow

on the witch's broom.

# On Halloween

BY JANE YOLEN

One bag of nuts,

Two chocolate bars,

Six sugar cookies cut like stars,

Four candy apples,

A raisin cluster—

Halloween's a tummy buster.

Oh, candy corn,

why do you appear

only once a year?

# Sweet Tooth

BY CANDACE PEARSON

A handful
of loose teeth rattle
in my pocket,
triangles of orange
and yellow
bitten off just so,
nip by nip
to the white tip.

24

Door to door,
street to street,
happy tongue,
tired feet!

# Trick-or-Treating

BY MICHELE KRUEGER

Walk and knock,

walk and knock,

all the way

around the block.

# Going Ghosting

BY REBECCA KAI DOTLICH

Gloves and socks

and sheets of white

will dress us up

like ghosts tonight.

We'll BOO, we'll scare,

we'll be a pair

of floating *things*

in stocking feet,

softly moaning, *Trick*

*or Treat*, till every face

at every door, begs us PLEASE,

"No more, no more!"

# The Best Trick

BY SANDRA GILBERT BRÜG

The best trick

   on Halloween night,

      besides shouting,

      "BOO!"

Is wearing a mask

   so neighbors will ask,

# Night Delight

BY JOAN BRANSFIELD GRAHAM

Out in a night that is

dark and delicious,

smooth as chocolate,

sweet candy kisses,

dressed in our costumes,

we dance with delight

on this play-out-late,

stay-out-late, magical night!

Halloween hisses

Halloween shrieks—

Halloween spooks

whenever it speaks.

15

# Night Noises

BY MARIA FLEMING

Halloween howls

Halloween moans

Halloween rattles,

cackles, groans.

and suddenly—
a fairytale Queen
is all dressed up
for Halloween.

# Costume Hour

BY REBECCA KAI DOTLICH

Out of the box

fly tangled wigs.

Shoes. Pink shirts.

Ballerina skirts.


Pull out a rainbow

of plastic beads.

Grandmother's gown.

A paper crown,

His smile burns for me.

# My Pumpkin

BY CRAIG CRIST-EVANS

I carve his eyes, nose, teeth.

I cut his hat to fit his head.

For light I put a candle in.


Tonight we light him up.

Some will say he's frightening.

Some will say he's just okay, but


I don't care *what* they say.

My pumpkin is my pumpkin.

spookiest masks I've ever seen—

something's coming—

HALLOWEEN!

# Something's Coming

BY VIRGINIA KROLL

Smell of smoke

from wood-burning stoves,

ripe red apples,

crushed black cloves,

crunchy leaves of brown and gold,

pumpkins bigger than I can hold,

# CONTENTS

*To*
*Anne Hoppe—*
*who*
*howls*
*poetry*
*—L.B.H.*

*For Riley, who loves monsters*
*—S.S.*

ACKNOWLEDGMENTS

Thanks are due to the following for use of works that appear in this collection:

Sandra Gilbert Brüg for "The Best Trick." Used by permission of the author, who controls all rights.

Craig Crist-Evans for "My Pumpkin." Used by permission of the author, who controls all rights.

Curtis Brown, Ltd., for "Costume Hour" and "Going Ghosting" by Rebecca Kai Dotlich; copyright © 2005 by Rebecca Kai Dotlich. "12:01 A.M." by Lee Bennett Hopkins; copyright © 1993 by Lee Bennett Hopkins. "Sweet Tooth" by Candace Pearson; copyright © 2005 by Candace Pearson. "On Halloween" by Jane Yolen; copyright © 2005 by Jane Yolen. All used by permission of Curtis Brown, Ltd.

Maria Fleming for "Night Noises." Used by permission of the author, who controls all rights.

Joan Bransfield Graham for "Night Delight." Used by permission of the author, who controls all rights.

Virginia Kroll for "Something's Coming." Used by permission of the author, who controls all rights.

Michele Krueger for "Trick-or-Treating." Used by permission of the author, who controls all rights.

Natasha Wing for "Black Cat." Used by permission of the author, who controls all rights.

ISBN-13: 978-0-439-89912-3
ISBN-10: 0-439-89912-5

12 11 10 9 8 7 6 5 4 3 2 1          6 7 8 9 10 11/0

Printed in the U.S.A.                    23

First Scholastic printing, September 2006

I Can Read Book® is a trademark of HarperCollins Publishers Inc.

# An I Can Read Book™

# HALLOWEEN HOWLS

## Holiday Poetry

### selected by Lee Bennett Hopkins
### pictures by Stacey Schuett

SCHOLASTIC INC.
New York   Toronto   London   Auckland   Sydney
Mexico City   New Delhi   Hong Kong   Buenos Aires